Dennis M. Gormley

Dealing with the Threat of Cruise Missiles

Adelphi Paper **339**

Oxford University Press, Great Clarendon Street, Oxford OX2 6DP
Oxford New York
Athens Auckland Bangkok Bombay Calcutta Cape Town
Dar es Salaam Delhi Florence Hong Kong Istanbul Karachi
Kuala Lumpur Madras Madrid Melbourne Mexico City
Nairobi Paris Singapore Taipei Tokyo Toronto
and associated companies in
Berlin Ibadan

Oxford is a trade mark of Oxford University Press

Published in the United States
by Oxford University Press Inc., New York

© The International Institute for Strategic Studies 2001

First published June 2001 by **Oxford University Press** for
The International Institute for Strategic Studies
Arundel House, 13–15 Arundel Street, Temple Place, London WC2R 3DX
www.iiss.org

Director John Chipman
Editor Mats R. Berdal
Assistant Editor John Wheelwright
Project Manager, Design and Production Mark Taylor

British Library Cataloguing in Publication Data
Data available

Library of Congress Cataloguing in Publication Data

ISBN 0-19-851527-8
ISSN 0567-932x

Contents

Glossary

AAM	air-to-air missile
ADSAM	air-directed surface-to-air missile
ASCM	anti-ship cruise missile
AWACS	Airborne Warning And Control System
BMC³	battle-management command, control and communications
BMDO	Ballistic Missile Defense Organization
C³I	command, control, communications and intelligence
CASOM	conventionally armed stand-off missile
CEC	Cooperative Engagement Capability
CEP	circular error probable
CID	combat identification
DARPA	Defense Advanced Research Projects Agency
DGPS	differential GPS
DPG	Defense Planning Guidance
DSMAC	digital scene-matching area correlation
EADS	European Aeronautic, Defence and Space Company
FCS	fire-control system
FMC	flight-management computer
G-7	Group of Seven
Gb	gigabyte(s)
GLONASS	Global Navigation Satellite System
GPS	Global Positioning System
ICBM	intercontinental ballistic missile

INS	inertial navigation system
IR	infra-red
JASSM	Joint Air-to-Surface Stand-off Missile
JDAM	Joint Direct Attack Munition
JLENS	Joint Land-attack Cruise Missile Defense Elevated Netted Sensor System
JSTARS	Joint Surveillance Target Attack Radar System
JTAMDO	Joint Theater Air and Missile Defense Organization
LACM	land-attack cruise missile
LCCMD	Low Cost Cruise Missile Defense
MALD	Miniature Air Launched Decoy
Mb	megabyte(s)
MBD	Matra BAe Dynamics
MBT	main battle tank
MEADS	Medium Extended Air Defense System
MHz	megahertz
MSOW	modular stand-off weapon
MTCR	Missile Technology Control Regime
NAVSTAR	Navigation Satellite for Time and Ranging
NORAD	North American Air Defense Command
NTW	Navy Theater-Wide defense
PLA	People's Liberation Army
RCS	radar cross-section
RMA	revolution in military affairs
RPV	remotely piloted vehicle
RTIP	Radar Technology Insertion Program
SAM	surface-to-air missile
SIAP	single integrated air picture
SLAM	Stand-off Land-Attack Missile
TEL	transporter-erector-launcher
TERCOM	terrain contour matching
THAAD	Theater High-Altitude Area Defence
UAE	United Arab Emirates
UAV	unmanned aerial vehicle
UCAV	unmanned combat aerial vehicle
WMD	weapon(s) of mass destruction

Introduction

Ballistic missiles dominated the missile-proliferation scene through-out the last decade of the twentieth century. Yet, for land-attack missions, cruise missiles were more prominent instruments of warfare than ballistic missiles during that decade[1] – as witness the extensive US use of *Tomahawk* cruise missiles in seven different contingencies, including the Gulf War and the Kosovo campaign. Importantly, though, these weapons had not yet spread widely beyond the arsenals of the US and Russia.

Now, however, many analysts and defence planners predict that before long the developing world will exploit the ongoing scientific, economic and social transformations that are contributing to an emerging 'revolution in military affairs' (RMA) to develop significant quantities of cruise missiles. Even worse, weak export controls could permit direct purchases of advanced cruise missiles from major industrial suppliers. As Lawrence Freedman has observed, 'Cruise missiles ... are to some extent the paradigmatic weapon of the RMA, as delivery systems that can be launched from a variety of platforms and strike in a precise manner and with low collateral damage'.[2] If the use of large numbers of land-attack cruise missiles (LACMs) becomes a widespread and dominant feature of military operations in the twenty-first century, the strategic conse-quences for international security could be profound.

Cruise-missile Proliferation:
Strategic Context and Possible Consequences

The notion that LACMs could emerge to threaten US military dominance seems, on the surface, dubious. If anything, the US appears to be increasing the capability gap between itself and its allies as well as its adversaries. Nevertheless, the military-related technologies that lie behind the emerging military transformation are spreading too rapidly and too widely to justify relying on *Operation Desert Storm* as the principal yardstick for thinking about future warfare. Indeed, America's growing dominance in conducting conventional warfare makes it highly likely that potential adversaries will seek new means of thwarting military intervention, one of which may be the acquisition and deployment of cruise missiles. Thus, cruise-missile proliferation could make power projection increasingly risky.

Crucial to the outcome of any intervention is the strength of the adversary's determination to resist it in the first place – especially early on. Analysts of the Gulf War's military lessons generally agree that *Operation Desert Storm* proved the decisiveness of striking the first blow in modern conventional warfare.[3] Regional foes of American military supremacy have drawn important lessons from the Gulf War; among the most salient is that, no matter what kinds of weapons a regional power acquires to confront a US-led intervention, in the long run it will not prevail against a technologically superior superpower.[4] Nonetheless, a regional power, whose stake is likely to be higher than those of the intervening powers, can make the prospect of intervention so costly as to deter any action at all – particularly since the American military leadership has become fixated on justifying intervention largely, if not exclusively, on the grounds of military 'doability': the assurance of quick victory with minimal casualties. Future adversaries of American-led coalitions are unlikely to repeat Iraq's error of permitting an unimpeded force build-up over nearly six months and then ceding the timing of attack to US decision-makers. Moreover, US force reductions and the elimination of the Cold War 'overhang' only make matters worse. Without the luxury of an extensive overseas system of bases and lines of communication that proved so useful in the Gulf War, US military forces will be less capable of absorbing the shock of any successful enemy strikes. Simply put, because such future interventions are likely to face opposition from the start, they may be vulnerable to serious disruption, high-risk improvisation, significant casualties and problematic public support.

The emergence of LACMs to complement ballistic-missile strike systems could conceivably bolster a prospective adversary's willingness to oppose US-led interventions in strategically significant ways. However inaccurate Iraq's modified *Scuds* were in 1991, they still absorbed a substantial fraction of coalition air sorties and nearly brought Israel into the conflict. Had Saddam Hussein not conveniently given the US nearly six months to increase its August 1990 inventory of three experimental *Patriot* Advanced Capability Version 2 (PAC-2) missiles to a considerably larger – if questionably effective – number by the time *Scud* attacks began, coalition political solidarity might have been severely threatened. Adding LACMs to the threat picture gives states that wish to deter or affect the outcome of US-led interventions not just political but also important new military leverage. Compared with ballistic missiles, cruise missiles are expected to be much more accurate (by a factor of at least ten), less costly (by at least half) and, because of their aerodynamic stability, substantially more effective in delivering chemical or biological payloads (conservatively, enlarging the lethal area for biological attacks by at least ten times).[5] Against this backdrop, the emergence of precisely delivered attacks against key fixed points (ports, airfields and other logistical sites) must be anticipated. Such attacks could be used not just to harass but to achieve strategic leverage in the early phase of a major theatre campaign.

By no means, however, are regional campaign contingencies the only strategic context in which the cruise-missile threat figures. As the US considers options for deploying national missile defences against ballistic-missile threats, it must also confront alternative ways that enemies might wish to attack the US homeland. A ship-launched LACM, fired from outside territorial waters, could strike most of the population and industry in North America and Europe.

Defence against Cruise Missiles: The Military Challenge

According to Allied Supreme Commander Dwight D. Eisenhower, had the Germans managed to perfect their V-weapons six months earlier, the invasion of Europe might not been possible. That said, Britain did demonstrate unusual technical and operational innovation in rapidly improving its defences against the slow, high-flying V-1 cruise missile. During the last four weeks of V-1 attacks, air defences intercepted, respectively, 24%, 46%, 67% and 79% of incoming V-1s.[6] Yet roughly 21,000 V-1s were launched against the Allies during the war, causing more than 18,000 casualties in London alone.

But defending against today's LACMs is a more complicated challenge than the one that Britain faced from German V-1s, for two reasons:

- Most of today's missiles have sleek aerodynamic designs (and in many cases, are intentionally stealthy) and are therefore more difficult to detect than their predecessors.
- They can be designed to fly essentially earth-hugging flight profiles, using terrain features to avoid detection.

Both airborne and ground-based surveillance radars are greatly taxed by these twin realities. Reduced radar observability means that the defence has less time to react. Low flight complicates airborne surveillance due to ground clutter (radar returns from objects on the ground other than the target), which results in very high noise rates and insufficient signals from the real target to enable its presence to be detected. For ground-based radars, the earth's curvature limits the distance at which low-flying targets can be detected to just tens of kilometres.

To respond to the manned-aircraft threat, the US alone has invested many tens of billions of dollars in theatre air defences: fighter-based air-to-air missiles (AAMs), airborne surveillance aircraft, surface-to-air missiles (SAMs) and battle-management command, control and communications (BMC^3). Some of today's theatre air defences have substantial capability against large LACMs flying relatively high flight profiles, but, once cruise missiles fly low or (worse) add stealth features or employ endgame countermeasures (decoys or jammers), severe difficulties arise. Even against highly observable cruise missiles flying relatively high, radars could mistake friendly aircraft returning to their bases for these targets and inadvertently shoot them down. And when ballistic missiles are added to this threat picture, ground-based theatre defences would be doubly stressed trying to cope with both high- and low-angle missile threats.

The emergence of large numbers of weapons-carrying unmanned aerial vehicles (UAVs) flying at very slow speeds also threatens the utility of legacy air-defence systems. Today's expensive air-defence systems were designed to detect high-performance Soviet air threats flying at high speeds. Sophisticated look-down radars on today's legacy systems eliminate slow-moving targets on or near the ground, to prevent their data processing and display systems from being overtaxed, so large numbers of propeller-driven UAVs flying at under 80 knots would be ignored as potential targets.[7] Although ground-based SAM radars could detect such slow-flying threats, the limited radar horizon of ground-based radars, in conjunction with large raid size, means that the SAM batteries could be quickly overwhelmed and their missile inventories rapidly depleted.

Meeting the Cruise-missile Proliferation Threat: The Policy Challenge

If cruise-missile proliferation proceeds unimpeded and becomes widespread, it may combine with the further spread of ballistic missiles to give multidimensional offence a distinct advantage over layered defence – no matter how much is invested in such a defence.[8] Accordingly, assessing how the cruise-missile proliferation threat could evolve is essential to making appropriate choices about how best to respond to it. The three key dimensions of this evolution are its pace, quality and quantity. Unlike the ballistic-missile threat – which has emerged quantitatively and qualitatively in a slow, sequential fashion – LACMs conceivably could spread not only quickly but also non-sequentially, including both early designs with large radar observables and advanced missiles with stealth features. This is because the 33-nation Missile Technology Control Regime (MTCR) is decidedly more effective at controlling ballistic missiles than cruise missiles. What is more, large numbers of cheap UAVs, target drones, or possibly even some anti-ship cruise missiles (ASCMs), could be converted into LACMs that could overwhelm much higher-cost defences.

Several different scenarios for cruise-missile proliferation must be considered. Because of relatively weak export controls affecting the acquisition of both cruise-missile components and complete systems, countries interested in developing them have a variety of sources to turn to.

- Indigenous development is not only the longest route to acquiring militarily significant cruise-missile capabilities; it is also unlikely to lead developing states to true autarky or anything beyond low-tech designs. Foreign assistance is a critical variable affecting the pace and quality of indigenous cruise-missile development.

- Though often cited as a major concern, the conversion of significant numbers of short-range ASCMs into land-attack systems may actually have a low potential for driving proliferation. There is indeed a huge extant population of ASCMs world-wide, but closer analysis suggests that only a small proportion is suitable for conversion into systems with ranges over 300km.

- A more worrying proliferation source, as noted, is the conversion of unarmed UAVs, including reconnaissance and target drones. These are increasingly used not only in tactical military systems but also in non-military commercial, civic and scientific applications. Of the 40 nations indigenously producing UAVs today, only 22 are MTCR members.

- Clearly, the cheapest means of acquiring large numbers of cruise missiles is by transforming small kit aircraft into weapons-carrying, fully autonomous attack vehicles – in effect, a 'poor man's cruise-missile arsenal'. There is a dizzying array of unregulated kit aircraft from which to build an inventory of slow-flying but difficult-to-detect 'missiles'.

- In some ways the easiest, and certainly the most worrying, way of acquiring highly sophisticated LACMs is simply to buy them from the growing list of world manufacturers. According to the US intelligence community, at least nine countries will be manufacturing LACMs in the next decade, and, without improved export controls, many such missiles could end up being exported to non-MTCR members.[9]

Argument in Brief

This Adelphi Paper illuminates how the cruise-missile proliferation threat may unfold and examines its strategic consequences. It argues that, precisely because the unfolding pattern of the cruise-missile threat remains so unclear and has not emerged as quickly as some analysts have predicted, more must be done now to develop and implement hedging strategies that could dissuade adversaries from acquiring them or delay the threat's emergence.

Effective hedging strategies must take into account both the utility and the necessity of cruise missiles to a potential user. Motivation for acquiring LACMs is based at least in part on perceived military utility – particularly where the targeted state's vulnerability interacts closely with the precision of attack to produce significant military payoff. Determining their utility to a given user requires consideration of the operational uses and effectiveness of cruise missiles armed with conventional weapons and weapons of mass destruction (WMD) payloads in various possible circumstances. The attractiveness of cruise missiles also turns on competing military needs, as determined by regional contexts, resource constraints, the feasibility of military alternatives (not least ballistic missiles), opponent countermeasures and the challenges of assimilating cruise missiles into existing force structures.

Any truly comprehensive hedging strategy would have to forge a much tighter link than presently exists between military solutions and more effective non-proliferation policies. Defence choices involve establishing priorities and making trade-offs between theatre and homeland requirements, though improvements in the former feed naturally into the latter. Theatre-defence needs ought to take precedence over homeland ones, if only because it is in various regional settings that cruise-missile threats are likely first to emerge overtly, and quite possibly in large numbers, to threaten US global presence. One immediate priority would be to strengthen current air defences against existing and near-term threats by providing a common air picture to distinguish friends from foes. In this connection, making such a common air picture available to close allies would make good sense. Such strategies might also entail modestly funded, but well coordinated technology development programmes to support the future deployment of highly effective defences against more sophisticated threats. But it is not just sophisticated cruise missiles that are of concern over the longer run. The prospect of large low-cost raids gives impetus to the search for much lower-cost alternatives than simply proliferating high-cost legacy air defences. Equally imperative are improvements in counter-force operations against ground launchers and supporting infrastructure. While these strategies do not require technological breakthroughs, they do involve an extraordinary degree of military service interoperability, as well as changes in existing bureaucratic, organisational and doctrinal practices. None of these changes will occur without sustained national leadership.

Non-proliferation policy is the first line of defence, but perhaps the least effective one at present. Missile non-proliferation policy focuses almost entirely on controlling the spread of ballistic missiles. Not nearly enough is being done to correct the gaping deficiencies in the way MTCR member-governments handle transfers of cruise-missile systems and technology. Using the mechanisms already in place in the MTCR, more effective implementation policies could greatly reduce the cost of defences against cruise missiles.

Uncertainty about the threat of cruise-missile proliferation has furnished a convenient rationale for careless exaggeration, on the one hand, and excessively cautious behaviour (or no action at all), on the other hand. Exaggeration is reflected in faulty assumptions about the ease of acquiring modern cruise missiles (or converting anti-ship ones) and the irrelevance of export controls to slowing their spread. More careful appraisal suggests that most developing countries will need considerable time and foreign assistance to produce militarily significant quantities of cruise missiles, especially stealthy ones. Assimilating cruise missiles effectively into force structures also takes more time than it does for ballistic missiles. On the other hand, hardly any serious attention has focused on the spread of converted UAVs, particularly those that fly so slowly that they overwhelm sophisticated air defences. As for the MTCR being irrelevant to the pace and scope of the threat's emergence, this need not be the case. The regime has made acquiring ballistic missiles more costly and complex. Given a greater consensus on cruise-missile controls among MTCR members, at least direct sales of highly advanced cruise missiles and related stealth and counter-measure technologies might be avoided. This would make threat calculations and defence planning more predictable by forcing proliferating states to take much longer paths to acquiring sophisticated cruise missiles. As for excessive policy caution or inaction, these are fraught with danger. Without a comprehensive set of hedging strategies to link strengthened non-proliferation measures with judicious choices in cruise-missile defence preparedness, the cruise-missile threat will emerge to jeopardise US and allied security interests and regional military balances.

Chapter 1

Technological Challenges of Acquiring LACMs

Growing concern over the proliferation of LACMs is largely driven by the quantum leap in technologies underlying their development. A week before Christmas 2000, an article on the Internet stated that the US intelligence community was concerned that Iraq might have acquired some 4,000 Sony *PlayStation* 2 video games.[1] This report, of course, became the subject of parody on American television's Jay Leno Show, but it does have its serious side. Each *PlayStation* 2 contains a 300 MHz, 128-bit processor, plus a graphics package five times more powerful than today's typical graphics workstation. The intelligence community's concern was that a bundled configuration of 12–15 of these units provides enough computer power to control the flight of a UAV. Iraq is believed to have transformed a number of Czech L-29 training aircraft into UAVs capable of delivering a payload of 200kg from a distance of over 600km.[2]

Facetious or not, the story exemplifies the simple truth that the commercial marketplace has dramatically altered the non-proliferation setting that faces today's security planners. Indeed, even comparatively primitive computer technology, like an Intel 486-class chip, equipped with 16Mb of random-access memory (half of one *PlayStation* 2's RAM) and a 1Gb hard drive, is sufficient to act as a modern cruise missile's flight-management computer: the hub of its crucial navigational controls.[3] Over and above the dramatically increased and miniaturised computing power, it is the widespread availability of cheap guidance, navigation, high-resolution satellite imaging and digital mapping technologies that is most responsible for raising the prospect of cruise-missile proliferation.

Key Enabling Technologies

The first cruise missiles were adapted from drones or manned aircraft and, like today's modern designs, consisted of four major parts: airframe, payload, guidance and propulsion. Guidance and propulsion represent the two major barriers to the spread of LACMs. Early designs used standard liquid-fuelled aircraft engines and autopilots for guidance and control. Later on, command guidance schemes and, more broadly, inertial navigation systems (INS), replaced autopilots, and solid propellants and air-breathing engines (turbojets at first) largely supplanted liquid-propelled engines. But the long flight times of these early cruise missiles meant that INS accumulated operationally unacceptable navigation errors, resulting from inertial drift, wind and thermal up-drafts, and did not permit cruise missiles to fly low, evading terrain obstructions, and thereby avoid enemy radar detection and active defences.

Around 1970 these problems were ameliorated with the development of a new guidance technology known as terrain contour matching (TERCOM).[4] This uses miniature radar in the missile's nose to sense the terrain over which it is flying and compares it with mapping data stored in the flight-control system. TERCOM thus provides course corrections that permit more accurate delivery of the missile's payload and facilitates very low-level flight to help the missile avoid enemy air defences. An even more sophisticated guidance scheme – digital scene-matching area correlation (DSMAC) – has subsequently further improved cruise-missile accuracy. These developments ushered in a plethora of new types of cruise missiles, notably the US *Tomahawk*.

So long as TERCOM and DSMAC represented the state of the art, there were three important barriers to proliferation. First, the functionality of these technologies depended on maps derived from highly classified overhead reconnaissance satellites. Second, developing a dedicated mapping infrastructure was prohibitively expensive. Third (and perhaps most important) TERCOM and DSMAC were subject to strong export controls.

New Proliferation Vulnerabilities

Guidance Systems

The advent of the Global Positioning System (GPS) has had the most profound effect: it has reduced the primary technical barriers to entering the LACM business.[5] When conceived by the US military after the Vietnam war, GPS – formally known as Navigation Satellite for Time and Ranging (NAVSTAR) – was intended only for military customers, primarily for the straightforward purpose of helping soldiers, sailors and airmen keep their bearings and avoid enemy detection. The $5bn system (the largest constellation of military satellites yet deployed) consists of 24 primary and four spare vehicles operating in six different polar orbital planes approximately 20,200km high. This positioning ensures that users on the earth can observe at least six satellites at any given time. Signals from three satellites are needed to achieve a precise two-dimensional position, while four satellites are required for a three-dimensional fix; receipt of signals from more than four satellites only increases the accuracy of the fix.[6]

Military uses of GPS abound. The Gulf War offered the US military a showcase for several GPS applications, when over 9,000 hand-held units, most of them commercially acquired, were distributed to US units. While Iraqi units were operating blindly in the featureless desert, US units gained great advantage from navigating accurately. GPS permitted the plotting of safe lanes through minefields and effective registration and aiming of artillery and rocket fire. Since the Gulf War *Tomahawk* cruise missiles have been upgraded with GPS receivers, obviating dependence on expensive satellite imagery data and lengthy mission-planning cycles. Moreover, as demonstrated in the Kosovo air campaign, the US has transformed unguided free-fall (dumb) bombs into highly lethal 'smart' weapons by including a low-cost integrated INS/GPS guidance kit in the Joint Direct Attack Munition (JDAM).[7]

After the Soviet destruction of Korean Air Lines Flight 007 over the Kamchatka Peninsula in 1983, President Reagan decided to make GPS widely and freely available globally, to help to avoid future air disasters. Since then civilian applications of GPS have grown in fits and starts. In 1990, the US Department of Defense instituted a policy of 'selective availability', intentionally inserting subtle errors into the GPS code used by civilians. Ways to work around selective availability quickly developed, however. The technique known as Differential GPS (DGPS) uses ground-based radio beacons to correct for errors, often producing navigational fixes better than those provided by the Pentagon's restricted code. Thus, in May 2000, President Clinton ended the selective availability programme, and civilian GPS receivers, once accurate to within 100m, can now operate typically at about 15m.

Russia also has deployed a GPS-equivalent called Global Navigation Satellite System (GLONASS).[8] The commercial market has created integrated GPS/GLONASS receivers that in tests by Honeywell and Northwest Airlines have shown positional fixes with accuracies consistently under 20m. Using combined GPS/GLONASS receivers to guide cruise missiles minimises degradation in GPS signal quality or accuracy. The low-cost commercial availability of INS with GPS or GLONASS allows developing nations to leap ahead roughly 15 years in navigation development with a single purchase.[9]

Commercial satellite imagery, though less consequential to proliferation than GPS, still is an important enabling technology for LACMs. A new generation of non-military observation satellites has begun to offer imagery products with performance characteristics that greatly exceed the US Landsat and French SPOT satellite systems. Imagery with a spatial resolution of less than 5m is now widely available. And, due to a US presidential decision in March 1994 that broadly reduces export controls on the sale of previously highly classified spy satellite technology and products, over the next few years several commercial satellites will begin to offer imagery with a resolution of 1m. Such commercial satellites will not deliver imagery as quickly as military reconnaissance systems do, but this will not limit their utility for supporting the targeting of LACMs – this can be accomplished in methodical fashion well before missiles are ever employed in combat.[10]

GPS and new commercial satellite imagery together can enhance mission planning for cruise missiles. Using an integrated GPS/INS approach to guiding a cruise missile obviates the need to make the detailed digital maps that TERCOM mission planning demands. On the other hand, most countries interested in cruise missiles for land-attack missions will want to improve the weapons' penetration and survivability by flying very low routes to the target, especially during the terminal phase of flight. Sophisticated Western aircraft employ expensive terrain-avoidance radars for this purpose, but these are not needed if accurate terrain elevation data can be programmed into the cruise missile in advance. Commercial products for such mission-planning tasks are now readily available; they consist of high-resolution imagery of the expected route to the target area, DGPS data and geographic information systems (computer hardware and software) that permit integration of GPS data into map products.

Indeed, assuming that an adversary could collect highly accurate DGPS positional data on major reference features en route to prospective targets (which requires physical access to these 'way points'), a TERCOM-like guidance system for intermediate and terminal guidance – all without depending on GPS or GLONASS updates – appears feasible. DGPS positional data, collected in peacetime, would be added to digitised satellite imagery to create a pre-programmed strip map used in conjunction with a radar altimeter to guide the cruise missile to its intended target.[11] It is important to keep in mind that the biggest difficulty in developing the TERCOM guidance technique has much less to do with the technological sophistication of TERCOM itself than with the mapping infrastructure it needs. This extensive and costly infrastructure stemmed from the US need to plan for a wide variety of world-wide contingencies, including thousands of different targets. By comparison, a regional power's requirements would more likely be confined to a much smaller target set for cruise-missile strikes.

Propulsion Systems

Whereas all the key enabling technologies for cruise-missile guidance and control are now readily available, those for advanced propulsion systems are not. It remains difficult for regional powers to manufacture or acquire gas-turbine engines required for LACMs with ranges above 300km.[12] China, for example, has produced the WP-11 turbojet engine for its HY-4 ASCM, but has had to rely on Russian technical support to produce advanced turbofan designs.[13] Such countries as India, Israel, South Africa and Taiwan are currently developing small turbojet engines that produce high thrust levels at the expense of fuel efficiency, and these could conceivably support cruise missiles capable of ranges up to 1,000km. For the foreseeable future, though, the manufacture of highly advanced turbofan designs is likely to remain limited to the US and Russia.

That does not mean, however, that advanced turbofan engines cannot be acquired for cruise-missile applications in relatively small lots. The Williams turbofan engine that powers the US *Tomahawk* cruise missile is export-restricted. But Williams also produces the FJ-44 and the newer FJ-44-2, civil versions of its military counterpart, for use in such commercial aircraft as the Cessna Citation and others. These versions produce a thrust that places them just outside the control of the MTCR.[14] Eventually, therefore, perhaps as many as 200 used Williams turbofan engines could become available for purchase in the surplus market. Although such advanced engine designs will not be available in large numbers, prospective proliferators could use other unrestricted turbojet engines produced by Britain, France, China, Russia, Japan, Canada and several other countries. In fact, the most widely proliferated turbojet engine is likely to be the one that propels various versions of the US-exported *Harpoon* anti-ship missile, which has already been transferred to 23 nations in Europe (including NATO allies), the Middle East (including Iran), the Far East and South America.

Finally, some countries might convert non-weaponised UAVs into LACMs. Such vehicles do not require anything like an advanced gas-turbine engine to achieve one-way ranges of over 1,000km. In fact they are far more likely to be powered by simple and cheap propeller-driven engines than by more modern gas-turbine engines.

Basic Prerequisites for Cruise-missile Development

Knowledge and skills as well as technology are required to manufacture cruise missiles indigenously from scratch, or to convert existing ASCMs or non-weaponised UAVs into LACMs. Also required is systems engineering capability. Arguably, what separates the industrial from the developing world is the capacity to integrate technology components into complex systems. If a nation seeks to acquire a small number of inaccurate, unreliable missiles, it can do so in a relatively straightforward and perfunctory fashion. Thus, the 1998 Commission to Assess the Ballistic Missile Threat to the United

States (known as the Rumsfeld Commission, after its chairman, the current US Secretary of Defense, Donald Rumsfeld) concluded that countries like North Korea and Iran could compress the development of long-range ballistic missiles into a much shorter time than it took either the US or Soviet Union to accomplish.[15] But producing significant quantities of highly effective cruise missiles calls not only for access to commercially available components but also for indigenous or foreign-provided systems-engineering talent.

Aeronautical engineering skills would be needed to make the fundamental calculations for the aerodynamic design of the air vehicle, and to create the hard data and algorithms needed for software inputs to the missile's critical flight-management computer – the heart of the modern low-flying cruise missile. Electrical engineering skills would be needed too, especially to integrate all the missile's electronic systems and its power supply. Computer programming skills have become crucially important because of the cruise missile's reliance on digital imagery, and its dependence on software to link the flight-management system's computer with the missile's flight controls. Mechanical machining and fitting skills are needed to install and custom fit structural members of the missile. Last but not least, an operational understanding of missile testing would be vital. A particular concern would be to develop a test programme that could verify the performance and reliability of the missile's avionics package, including its algorithms, and the structural alterations and aerodynamic modifications made during the missile's development. In essence, such tests would mimic problems that could conceivably occur during actual combat flight.

These basic intellectual prerequisites for cruise-missile development have both indigenous and foreign sources. Universities provide an excellent source for many of the needed skills; major universities in the developing world frequently include faculty and students educated at the best western universities specialising in engineering and computer science. Also, the number of foreign-trained scientists and engineers residing in the developing world nearly doubled between 1972 and 1992.[16] Although foreign nationals might only be temporary, and many would be vigilant about disclosing information that might affect their home countries' security, some could still furnish extremely valuable, first-hand experience to allies or ostensibly neutral states if they had worked on advanced cruise-missile designs in their home countries. The disposition of technical personnel from the former Soviet Union remains a continuing non-proliferation concern; the Chinese have recruited a large team of Russian technical personnel to assist in their cruise-missile programmes.[17]

Civilian and military industries would certainly also represent useful sources of skills. A manufacturing base for light aircraft would offer skills needed to fabricate cruise-missile airframes. Signature reduction is another matter. While simple airframe shaping to reduce the missile's radar cross-section is conceivable, more advanced techniques involving special materials are far more difficult to achieve. Critical systems integration and engineering skills could be developed from an automotive industry, and over time applied to comparable cruise-missile integration tasks. For example, Iran has integrated several fairly complex foreign components into the *Safir*-74 (its upgrade of the Soviet-era T-54/55 tank), including a computerised fire-control system.[18] Iran also has plans to develop an even more sophisticated main battle tank (MBT), the *Zolfaqar* MBT.[19] Workers from blossoming electronics, telecommunications and computer industries could also contribute key programming, design and testing skills. India's sudden emergence as a leading venue for computer software design and manufacture may be exceptional, nonetheless other lesser examples can make important contributions to cruise-missile development.

Country-specific Proliferation Potential

The pace at which a developing country might be able to harness component technologies and needed integration skills to produce LACMs will be driven by two key variables: the scope and sophistication of indigenous skills and the level of foreign assistance. While considerable variation exists from country to country, there are clear indicators of greater or lesser potential. A country that possessed only rudimentary aeronautical experience, based entirely on its commercial airports, and no significant supporting industrial capabilities from which to draw needed engineering talent, would have a very low potential for acquiring a cruise-missile capability. By contrast, a state with high potential would have a few well-respected technical universities, an established automotive industry, emerging electronics and computer industries, and at least a limited aviation development and production industry, with manufacturing or modification of commercial and military aircraft, or a significant familiarity with foreign commercial and military aircraft. Such a state could be expected to contribute in important ways to the development and integration of the cruise missile's avionics package. Incremental advantages would flow to developing countries fitting somewhere in between these two extremes. These might possess a fledgling electronics or automotive industry, a national technical university, modest to well-developed commercial and military aviation infrastructures and even some modest experience with regularly exercising and maintaining modern military aircraft. 'States of concern' in terms of cruise-missile proliferation are those in the latter two categories.

High-potential Countries
India furnishes an example of a developing nation with significant indigenous potential to produce LACMs. India has not, it should be noted, reached a stage of self-reliance in defence production. For the vast majority of its defence projects it still depends on licensed production from foreign sources to produce major weapon systems.[20] On the other hand, the country does have experience of manufacturing military and dual-use aircraft of indigenous and foreign design. Skills and knowledge, especially important systems-integration experience, come not only from its nuclear weapons programme but also from the development of indigenously produced ballistic missiles.

India's current inventory of cruise missiles is limited to anti-ship systems, but there appears to be growing support for both the acquisition and the indigenous development of LACMs.[21] As part of its deal to procure two *Kilo*-class submarines from Russia, India is expected to receive Russian 3M-54E *Club* cruise missiles, which are believed to have both anti-ship and land-attack capabilities. But it has also shown a willingness to produce its own LACM, the *Lakshya* – based on an unmanned target drone, this reportedly will carry a 450kg payload to a range of 600km, guided and controlled by a combined GPS/INS system accompanied by either a radar or infra-red (IR) terminal seeker. Moreover, India is seeking to develop a new engine for the *Lakshya*, which would replace its French-designed turbojet.[22] Successful indigenous development of such an engine could extend the missile's range and represent an important achievement in military design and engineering.

Like India, South Africa (an MTCR member-state) has shown significant potential for defence industrial production, having developed and produced a small arsenal of nuclear weapons, which was subsequently destroyed with the collapse of apartheid. Over the last several years South Africa has begun development of, and heavily marketed, both small UAVs and LACMs. The *Flowchart 2* turbojet-driven target drone is perhaps the most interesting development, in that it features a very clean, stealthy design and extensive use of composite materials in its construction. The South Africans have also marketed two new developmental cruise missiles: *MUPSOW* and *Torgos*, both of which are slated to come in either air- or ground-launched versions. *Torgos* appears to have several advanced features – including an imaging IR terminal seeker and digital data link for guidance and control, automatic target recognition and an optional low-light TV camera for terminal engagements – which combine to give a claimed accuracy of 2m circular error probability (CEP). Powered by a turbojet engine, *Torgos* has an advertised range of 300km and a payload of 500kg.[23]

Medium-potential Countries

Though it does not have the technological infrastructure of India or South Africa, Iran may well be in a position to undertake development of a LACM. It produces UAVs and has applied some to land-attack missions, and there are hints that the Iranian military is working on a 400km-range cruise missile.[24] To secure energy supplies in the Gulf and check American power, China may be willing to provide Iran with engineering assistance and experience gained from developing LACMs over the last 20 or more years.[25] Most US concerns seem to centre on the possibility of Iranian–Chinese collusion over building a facility in Iran for manufacturing copies of the Chinese C-801 and C-802 ASCMs.[26] The C-801 carries a small warhead and flies to only up to 40km; extending this to the range needed for land-attack missions would require removing its solid-propellant motor and replacing it with a turbojet engine. A more promising candidate is the C-802, which already has a turbojet engine and greater range capability (120km); Iran could conceivably scale up the C-802. Alternatively, it could convert its HY-2 *Silkworm* anti-ship missiles into longer-range land-attack systems by changing their solid-propellant engines for turbojets and replacing their anti-ship guidance system with a completely new land-navigation system. This would be technologically much more demanding, but the HY-2's large size and internal volume offer space for additional fuel, and hence extended range.

Although UN Security Council sanctions currently restrict Iraq's ability to obtain the assistance needed to continue developing its cruise-missile development programmes, Saddam Hussein still harbours hegemonic ambitions. Moreover, cracks in the sanctions regime that emerged in the late 1990s make Iraq's past attempts to develop LACMs more ominous. As already noted, Baghdad has converted an L-29 trainer into a weapon-carrying UAV; it has extended the range of its *Scud* and Soviet-supplied SS-N-2 *Styx* ASCMs by lengthening their airframes and adding fuel; and before the Gulf War it had a development programme to convert the Italian *Mirach* 600 reconnaissance UAV into the *Ababil* LACM, reportedly with a range of 500km and a payload of 450kg.[27] Of course, Iraq's prospects for manufacturing LACMs depend heavily on two factors: first, the extent to which bombing and subsequent UN inspections destroyed or dismantled supporting aerospace infrastructure; and second, the future status of UN sanctions.

Countries with more modest, yet still noteworthy, indigenous infrastructures are North Korea and Pakistan. North Korea is unique in that, while overall its economy is in shambles, it has nonetheless managed to maintain a modest self-sufficiency in assembling and producing several types of Soviet-era and Chinese weapon systems. It has also reverse-engineered the *Scud* missile into substantially longer-range systems. North Korea possesses several varieties of Soviet and Chinese ASCMs, has developed the capacity to produce the Chinese HY-2 *Silkworm* missile both for internal use and for export, and has acquired UAVs from European sources. Scaling up the range of ASCMs appears to be a North Korean goal. In 1994 US officials stated that Pyongyang had tested a 160km-range ASCM:

most likely an improved version of the HY-2 or HY-4.[28] If China has provided the turbojet-equipped HY-4 to North Korea, Pyongyang would have a useful building block for transforming the *Silkworm* into a land-attack missile.

Pakistan buys, rather than builds, most of its military equipment, which includes a modest inventory of Chinese (HY-2 *Silkworm*), US (*Harpoon*) and French (*Exocet*) ASCMs, and some reconnaissance UAVs from South Africa or China. With extensive foreign assistance, it has created the Pakistan Aeronautical Complex, which provides maintenance and overhaul services for foreign-supplied Pakistani aircraft. Pakistan also now indigenously produces the *Mushshak* training and observation aircraft, but its inherent capacity to design, develop and produce LACMs will depend heavily, if not exclusively, on China.

Foreign Assistance: Still the Chief Factor

In many respects, the notion of truly indigenous manufacture of LACMs by countries not possessing first-tier industrial status is mythical.[29] Most of the countries mentioned above are capable of license producing major weapon systems, but they depend critically on outside foreign assistance. Of course, as the Rumsfeld Commission noted, 'Foreign assistance is not a wild card. It is a fact.'[30] Nonetheless, it is important to remember that foreign assistance comes in many forms, ranging from elementary provision of drawings and a few technicians to the comprehensive provision of major sub-components (turbojet or turbofan engines), production equipment (tooling, machinery, test equipment) and senior engineering talent skilled in systems integration of complex military systems. The form of such assistance will greatly influence not just the possibility that a relatively advanced developing country might one day achieve a high degree of self-reliance in cruise-missile development, but also the speed with which recipient states convert ASCMs, unarmed UAVs and small aircraft into fully autonomous land-attack systems.

Chapter 2

Alternative Ways to Acquire LACMs

Assuming a state has a certain basic level of technological knowledge and capability, there are alternative ways (apart from indigenous development) by which it could acquire platforms suitable for developing LACMs. One would be to buy and convert ASCMs, UAVs and very light manned aircraft. The conversion process poses technological challenges, would take years, and in many cases would require considerable foreign assistance. Direct acquisition, on the other hand, requires no minimum indigenous technological capability and circumvents all conversion requirements – though, of course, it comes at the price of greater dependence on foreign suppliers. The primary constraint on proliferation by direct acquisition is the MTCR. Each of these proliferation avenues bears closer scrutiny.

Converting ASCMs into LACMs

US official concern about the cruise-missile threat centres mainly on the widespread proliferation of over 75,000 ASCMs. Indeed, both the US and Russia have demonstrated the potential of these weapons as platforms for building LACMs. The US Navy itself has transformed the ubiquitous *Harpoon* missile (AGM-84) – exported to 24 nations – into the Stand-off Land-Attack Missile (SLAM/AGM-84E).[1] Russia, too, is exploiting cruise-missile modularity in its export family of missiles called *Club*, which appears to have components from the 3M-55 *Yakhont* ASCM (NATO designation SS-NX-26).

The American and Russian conversions, however, are not broadly representative of what the developing world might do with existing inventories of ASCMs. Modern designs like the *Harpoon* and the *Club* tend to be smaller in volume than their land-attack cousins. They are also densely packed with integrated electronics and software, which leaves little room for changing engines, rearranging the guidance and control system and, most important, adding fuel. (Transforming the basic *Harpoon* into the SLAM did not alter the missile's relatively short range of 100km.[2]) For a developing nation interested in converting an ASCM, though, it would seem only logical (particularly in view of the costs of conversion) to want to deliver a fairly large payload (about 500kg) at least to a range of 300km, if not much further.

In contrast to *Harpoon* and *Club*, the Russian *Styx* and its Chinese derivative *Silkworm* are easier to modify, and, because of their roominess and simplicity of design, the conversion requires less technical skill. After the American *Harpoon* and French *Exocet*, the *Silkworm* and *Styx* together comprise probably the third largest class of exported ASCMs, appearing in the inventories of countries like Bangladesh, the Democratic Republic of Congo, Dubai, Egypt, Iran, Iraq, North Korea and Pakistan. With a total weight of around 2,500kg, the *Silkworm* is over 1,000kg heavier than the US *Tomahawk* missile (though its smaller and more modern cousin, the C-801, is one-third of this weight – and half the HY-2's width and three-fourths of its length). It appears feasible to greatly extend the *Silkworm's* current range of around 100km, as Iran, North Korea and Iraq are suspected of having done.[3]

Converting a *Silkworm* would require completely gutting its navigational system, which represents roughly 65% of its cost.[4] Given that developing the navigational system poses the greatest technological challenge involved in developing an LACM, indigenous development might seem a less wasteful alternative than acquiring *Silkworms*.[5] But the *Silkworm's* appeal resides mainly in its sheer size and ubiquity: its size provides room for substantial expansion of range and payload, while its ubiquity presents the opportunity of exploiting surplus missiles in a nation's inventory. If a country in the midst of upgrading its anti-ship missile inventory to HY-4s had surplus old HY-1s or HY-2s, they would furnish a useful starting point for conversion.[6] And other surplus anti-ship platforms without *Silkworm*'s volume might also provide attractive options for conversion, even if substantial range enhancement might not be feasible: a range of 200–300km is still significant in confined geographic areas like the Middle East and the Gulf.

Impediments to Converting ASCMs

There remain, however, significant barriers to converting *Silkworm*-class missiles into land-attack systems. First, a suitable turbojet engine must be found.[7] As of 2001, only one of the *Silkworm/Styx* family members, the Chinese HY-4, comes with a turbojet engine. With the exception of the developmental, ramjet-driven HY-3, all others have liquid-fuelled rocket engines, which makes them unsuitable for any significant range enhancement. Of course, one could choose to replace the liquid-rocket engine with a suitable turbojet engine; China's WP-11, which powers the more modern HY-4, is a natural candidate, and unrestricted gas-turbine engines are also available in the civilian and military markets from Canadian, European, Japanese, US and other international producers. The easiest route, however, would be to acquire the HY-4, which China now offers for sale in the export market. This missile can be ground- or air-launched and can deliver a 500kg payload to a range of 150–200km. China is believed to have used the HY-4 airframe to develop a land-attack system.[8]

The second and more formidable barrier to *Silkworm* conversion is providing a modern land-attack navigation system.[9] The required modifications would pay some operational dividends: they would free enough internal space to extend the range of the HY-4 (or a turbojet-equipped HY-1 or HY-2) to at least 500km.[10] All the same, developing a new navigation system would be a highly complex undertaking. Components would first have to be procured; they include an INS, a single GPS or combined GPS/GLONASS receiver, a radar altimeter, an electronic servo system, a power supply and alternator and a flight-management computer. The INS keeps track of the missile's location and orientation; acceptable INS packages can be acquired for as little as $20,000. The combination of a GPS/GLONASS receiver would provide satellite data and system redundancy; several GPS/GLONASS receivers for commercial aircraft are available for under $6,000. A radar altimeter would be needed in to ensure the lowest flight path possible, especially in the terminal phase; highly accurate radar altimeters are available for around $2,500. Digitally controlled electronic servos are crucial for moving the missile's control surfaces based on commands from the flight-management computer. Power for the entire system would be provided by a bank of direct-current batteries charged by an alternator slaved to the turbojet engine. Together, the latter two subsystems could be assembled from commercial parts and cost no more than $2,000.

Serving as the hub of all of these components is the flight-management computer (FMC), which would monitor and integrate the GPS/GLONASS, INS, radar altimeter and engine data, monitor the fuel flow from different tanks, trim the missile's weight and balance, and operate its control surfaces. This could be based on an Intel 486 computer motherboard with about 16 megabytes of random access memory and a 1Gb hard drive, costing less than $2,000. Basic software would also need to be written to incorporate flight control laws, autopilot functions, onboard system monitoring and flight-path and course navigation.[11] To generate this software, a country would have to incur the one-time costs of acquiring needed hardware (a UNIX workstation) and software (for map planning and integration), costing in the neighbourhood of $150,000. Required imagery acquisition would entail a recurring, but quite manageable cost, particularly given the growing array of commercial satellite vendors. Although these component technologies and subsystems are reasonably available 'off the shelf' or from the civilian or military aircraft markets, it is a daunting task to integrate individually complex electronic subsystems into a working whole that achieves the consistently precise results demanded of a land-attack navigation system. Each component of the system would have to be fully tested, and the missile's electronics would have to be carefully resupported and reinforced to accommodate the rough handling of flight and off-road travel. There are conceivable shortcuts, of which the most attractive is to acquire commercially available UAV flight-control systems. These would furnish valuable insight into precisely how a fully integrated navigation and control system operates.

With some modest level of foreign assistance, consisting of engineering and technical advisers, a developing nation such as Iran would probably require between six and ten years to produce the kind of modifications to the *Silkworm* outlined here and to establish the capacity to manufacture significant quantities of missiles. This estimate includes time to achieve some modest level of overall system reliability, maintainability and logistical support, including integrating such a new system into an existing force structure with appropriate attention to new doctrine, tactics and training. With much more substantial foreign assistance, including experienced engineering support and advanced production equipment, that time could conceivably be cut in half.[12]

Converting Unarmed UAVs into LACMs

For any nation with the technological wherewithal to develop a sophisticated land-attack navigation system, a more attractive proliferation option than converting ASCMs may lie with adapting unarmed UAVs to weapons-carrying roles. Unprecedented use of UAVs for a wide variety of military applications during the 1999 Kosovo conflict demonstrated that, although both technological and doctrinal obstacles to their most effective use in combat remain, expansion of UAV roles for military applications is destined to continue.[13] The military market for UAVs in 1997 was $1.9bn and is expected to grow to around $3.8bn in 2004. By contrast, the civilian commercial, scientific and civic markets for UAV applications together were a paltry $80 million in 1997, expected perhaps to rise to $175m by 2004. But major market growth in the US civilian sector is expected, once legal roadblocks and current air-traffic-control constraints are eliminated as full digitisation occurs.[14]

Some UAVs already come with GPS/INS guidance packages, or with fire-control systems readily adaptable to pre-programmed flight instructions. This makes conversion a comparatively straight-forward task, and that is more feasible for a broader array of developing countries than anti-ship missile conversion. With 40 nations now producing unarmed UAVs, the potential for such transformations is already evident. As previously noted, the Indian *Lakshya* and South African *Flowchart* 2 cruise missiles are converted target drones. Italy has widely exported its *Mirach* family of remotely piloted vehicles (RPVs), some of which provide the foundation for longer-range LACMs. The turbojet-powered *Mirach* 100, capable of delivering a 70kg payload to a range of 900km, has been exported to

Argentina, Iraq and Libya, and the *Mirach* 600 appears to be the basis for Iraq's development of the 450km-range *Ababil* LACM.[15] Israel is thought to be converting its own *Delilah* UAV into a 400km-range air-launched cruise missile for land attack, possibly in collaboration with China.[16]

Lower Barriers to UAV Conversion

Until recently, it was virtually impossible to appreciate in any systematic way the extent to which unarmed UAVs might become useful platforms for armed missions beyond ranges of 300km. This was largely due to the fragmentary and inconsistent nature of published information on relevant UAV range characteristics. Some manufacturers present the range of their UAVs as a figure limited by the line-of-sight radio data link that controls the vehicle's flight activities, others as a product of a loitering and return-to-base calculation; neither translates easily into the practical range of an armed cruise missile on a one-way mission. Further, many Chinese UAVs tend to have excess engine capacity that would extend useful range, and perhaps payload, capabilities much beyond the system's advertised specifications. Thus, using published UAV flight characteristics alone, it is impossible to determine for the great majority of systems whether or not they can reach a one-way range of at least 300km.

To help fill this gap in understanding UAVs, a 2000 study has revealed a new approach to estimating more accurately the true range potential of UAVs.[17] Briefly, the methodology takes existing fragmentary information from published materials and fits the data to an empirically driven aerodynamic model of flight behaviour.[18] The study developed a database of over 600 unarmed UAVs powered by either gas-turbine or reciprocating engines.[19] It demonstrated that without any modifications, such as changing engines or adding fuel bladders, nearly 80% of the unarmed UAVs have ranges in excess of 300km. Just as important, 65% have ranges over 500km, and 36% can fly beyond 1,000km. Although these UAV range values represent maximum ranges with minimal payloads (no modifications were assumed to trade range for increased payload), it is important to remember that UAVs' aerodynamic flight stability makes these vehicles well suited to delivering biological agents or small but highly effective packages of submunitions.[20]

Converting Very Light Manned Aircraft into Armed UAVs

Perhaps the fastest route to creating a 'poor man's' strategic arsenal is to convert small commercial aviation or kit aircraft into armed UAVs. Kit-aircraft packages come in many varieties, ranging from plans alone to complete kits. Generally, they do not include the reciprocating engine, which can be purchased separately but usually through the same manufacturer. Costing in the neighbourhood of $25,000 (including the engine), these small manned aircraft are based on proven, well-tested designs, many of which achieve high performance. A brief review of kit-aircraft literature suggests that there are numerous packages available for purchase with capabilities permitting one-way maximum ranges of around 1,000km, payloads of about 150kg, and very short take-off distances (100–200m) from grass fields.[21] Cruise speeds are generally around 120 knots, but these aircraft have stalling speeds low enough to permit them to fly at under 80 knots, thus making them more difficult to detect. Many come with folding wings, and most could be transported on small trucks for quick field set up, launch preparations, fuelling and subsequent launch.

Kit aircraft should be easier and cheaper to convert to autonomous land-attack systems than ASCMs. The pilot and passenger section of the aircraft would provide enough space for simple conversion to a payload section. As with ASCMs, the biggest challenge in converting kit planes lies in furnishing a suitable land-attack navigation system for fully autonomous flight as low as possible to the target. The job should be somewhat simpler to achieve, given the kit aircraft's rudimentary design, the manufacturer's provision of full engineering drawings and relevant aerodynamic data on the craft's flight performance, and the availability of full UAV flight-control systems ideally designed for such small aircraft. Of course, a nation interested in mass producing such a system would have to reverse-engineer these commercially provided components and technical data into a production system capable of stamping out reasonably reliable and maintainable units in large lots. Still, the kit plane's very simplicity suggests that the whole conversion process would be possible with substantially less foreign assistance than producing large numbers of converted ASCMs would be likely to involve.

The choice of adapting kit aircraft for weapons delivery may have particular appeal for a regional power confronting sophisticated Western air defences. High costs, limited inventories and poor performance against very-slow-flying threats characterise such air defences. While producing the land-attack navigation system would exceed the cost of acquiring the kit aircraft, when compared to any of the other UAV or anti-ship conversion options the overall cost would be such as to make saturation attacks quite conceivable. (Of course, the more appropriate comparison here is between large numbers of, say, $50,000-per-unit armed UAVs and limited inventories of missiles costing millions of dollars each.[22]) Moreover, converted kit aircraft, as well as other more expensive UAVs powered by reciprocating engines, could fly at such slow speeds – under 80 knots – that many sophisticated air-defence systems would, by design, simply ignore them as potential targets. Painted black, fitted with audio mufflers and launched to arrive after sunset, large numbers of these converted systems could seriously disrupt existing Western air defences.[23]

Acquiring LACMs from Industrial Suppliers

Each of the cruise-missile acquisition paths examined so far would require considerable time – and, more than likely, foreign assistance as well – to produce militarily significant numbers of LACMs. A quicker path would involve simply buying complete systems from a growing list of world suppliers. If dependence on a foreign supplier is not an impediment, direct purchase would be the fastest way of acquiring the most advanced, low-flying, stealthy cruise missiles – many with features equal to, and sometimes even greater than, those of current US LACMs. Until the mid- to late 1990s, the direct purchase of sophisticated LACMs was not very likely. Only the US and Russia were major producers, and Russia's prospects for significant export sales of such systems have not improved until very recently. What has changed the prospects for direct purchase is the fact that at least seven other countries have joined the list of producers, including several European nations, China, South Africa and Israel.

Evading the MTCR

Cruise missiles have several features that make it much more difficult to control their export under the provisions of the MTCR than to control ballistic-missile exports. From an engineering standpoint, cruise missiles can be adapted to increase range much more easily than ballistic missiles. The technology needed to produce a 1,000km-range cruise missile is not fundamentally different from that needed for much shorter-range systems. Depending on its payload and the amount and type of fuel used, range can frequently be improved by a factor of five or more without altering the cruise-missile airframe and engine.

Moreover, variations in cruise-missile flight profiles – especially taking advantage of more fuel-efficient flight at higher altitudes – can lead to substantially longer ranges than the cruise-missile manufacturers advertise. Evaluating ballistic missiles is relatively easy, because they are launched from one point on the ground to strike another, and their range is calculated on the basis of a maximum-range trajectory. By contrast, the large number of variables affecting cruise-missile range means that virtually each individual missile proposed for export would have to be considered on its own merits to determine whether MTCR provisions apply to it. Thus, while the MTCR has so far effectively contained the spread of advanced ballistic missiles, transfers of highly advanced cruise-missile systems are not as likely to be subject to MTCR controls. This shortfall in MTCR coverage renders cruise-missile threat calculations extraordinarily difficult to make. Unless MTCR controls on cruise-missile transfers are improved, highly advanced systems could appear in developing-world arsenals sooner than much less sophisticated indigenous designs or converted UAVs and ASCMs.

Russia and China

Russia began marketing LACMs in earnest during its premiere Moscow Air Show in 1992, when it offered for sale a shorter-range version of the 3,000km-range AS-15 (or Kh-55) air-launched cruise missile.[24] The missile's advertised range was 500km with a payload of 410kg, and its features included TERCOM-like guidance combined with GLONASS navigational updates, promising a terminal accuracy of less than 20m. A year later at the IDEX Defence Exhibition in Abu Dhabi, the Russians displayed a scaled-down AS-15, called the Kh-65E, with a range of 280km. These offerings demonstrate not only the inherent modularity of cruise missiles, but also a clumsy attempt by the Russian manufacturer Reduga to keep the offerings below the MTCR's range and payload thresholds. As previously noted, Russia has also exploited the modularity of its sea-launched 3M-55 *Yakhont* cruise missile to produce the 3M-54E1, or *Club*, for the export market. This missile is believed to have both anti-ship and land-attack options built in. India has already agreed to purchase the *Club* for deployment on its diesel submarines, and China, too, has reportedly expressed interest.[25] Russia clearly has strong pretensions to market cruise missiles aggressively, although a potential sales impediment – besides MTCR restrictions – may be its poor reliability as a supplier of technical service and spare parts. Clearly, however, Russia appears willing to put foreign markets ahead of internal ones, and this could indicate a concomitant willingness to address support issues more effectively.

Most of China's efforts to develop LACMs were not subject to public scrutiny until the late 1990s.[26] Relying in part on extensive Russian assistance, China is believed to have at least three new LACMs already deployed or under development. Beginning in the late 1970s, China experimented with precursor test beds and began developing small turbofan engines. Besides Russian assistance, China probably gained access to, and perhaps benefited from, the reverse-engineering of at least one of several intact US *Tomahawk* missiles recovered by Pakistan during the 1990s. By 1992 China deployed the *Hong Niao* 1 (HN-1) LACM with features indicative of a Russian pedigree. The HN-1 looks like the Russian AS-15, having the distinctive rear-mounted engine and under-body air intake; its range, payload and guidance characteristics also mimic the Russian KH-65E, the shorter-range variant of the AS-15. The HN-2 upgrade, first produced in 1996, reportedly has a range of between 1,500 and 2,000km. A further upgrade (HN-3), with a range of 2,500km, is under development. These developments, along with Chinese ballistic-missile acquisition, represent an increasingly potent threat against Taiwan. They also prompt concern about potential export sales, especially in light of China's questionable behaviour regarding past ballistic-missile transfers.

New Exporters

Over the last decade European manufacturers of LACMs have leapt to the top rung of world producers, led by the Anglo-French firm, Matra BAe Dynamics (MBD).[27] MBD is now believed to have at least $2.1bn-worth of development and early-production contracts and orders for over 2,000 of its LACMs, which come in three major variants. All these variants derive from the original French cruise-missile programme, called *Apache*. The *Apache* was informally conceived in 1987, when France decided not to participate in the multinational modular stand-off weapon (MSOW) programme, but instead to pursue its own independent development programme to meet French Air Force requirements for 500 missiles.[28] Formally under development since 1989, the *Apache* family of missiles is also modular in design; all its variants, from the shortest to the longest ranges, use the same basic airframe. Regardless of range, the *Apache* and its variants feature a stealthy aerodynamic shape, low-observable materials, low IR signatures and a combination of guidance and navigation schemes designed to achieve a high probability of survival and high terminal accuracy.

The shortest-range variant, still called the *Apache*, has a nominal range of 140km carrying a payload of anti-runway submunitions weighing around 520kg. The French Air Force is scheduled to receive 100 *Apaches*, with the first order of 25 arriving in 2001. A longer-range variant, called the *Storm Shadow*, won the UK conventionally armed stand-off missile (CASOM) competition in 1996, which brought about the decision to merge Matra and the missiles arm of BAe. A highly effective LACM with a range in the neighbourhood of 300–400km, the *Storm Shadow* is supported by a UK Ministry of Defence contract of roughly $1.3bn to equip Royal Air Force *Tornados* and *Eurofighters* and Royal Navy *Harriers*. The UK order is believed to be for more than 500 missiles. The French plan to acquire 500 *SCALP-EG* versions of the missile, ordered in 1997 by the French Ministry of Defence to equip *Mirage* 2000D and *Rafale* aircraft.[29] It is not precisely clear what the range of the *SCALP-EG* will be, but earlier French plans called for a 'strategic' version called *SCALP*, reserved exclusively for French use, that would have a range of 400–600km and very sophisticated stealth features.[30]

Robust exports of various versions of the *Apache* family of cruise missiles could favourably affect unit costs for French and UK missile buys. In October 1999 Italy joined the development programme and agreed to purchase the *Storm Shadow* variant for its *Tornados* and *Eurofighters*. And, as part of its decision to purchase 15 *Mirage* 2000-5 Mk2 fighters from Dassault, Greece has also decided to buy the *Storm Shadow*. Because Greece is an MTCR member-country, a transfer within the MTCR membership is far less contro-versial than one to a non-member-country.[31] The most troubling transaction so far, however, occurred in 1998, when the United Arab Emirates (UAE), a non-MTCR country, announced that it would receive an *Apache* derivative called *Black Shaheen*. The announcement drew a rash of formal and informal protests by Washington to London and Paris. (The US State Department believes that all versions of the *Apache* can carry a payload of at least 500kg to a range of at least 300km, and that Britain and France should therefore exercise a strong presumption to deny any exports to non-MTCR states.[32]) The protests apparently have not dissuaded Paris and London, however, as plans to make deliveries of *Black Shaheen* in 2003–04 remain unchanged.

While MBD clearly leads the way in developing and selling new LACMs, other European countries have entered the market as well. From the standpoint of technical sophistication, most prominent is the joint German/Swedish *Taurus* family of LACMs. Modular in design, the longest-range version of *Taurus* is believed to have a range of 350km and a payload roughly comparable to MBD's *Apache*. Like *Apache*, *Taurus* has highly advanced guidance and navigation, but, instead of depending on *Apache's* stealthy features, it can be equipped with endgame countermeasures (towed decoys, for example) to make it highly survivable.[33]

The most important Middle Eastern country to enter the cruise-missile development business is Israel. Responding to Greece's plans to acquire the *Storm Shadow*, Turkey has expressed interest in Israel's *Popeye* cruise missile, an air-launched system with a range of over 300km.[34] In addition to Israel's various overt development activities with shorter-range cruise missiles, rumours abound that Israel test launched a long-range cruise missile from a submarine in the Indian Ocean sometime in 2000. Although Israeli government officials have denied such reports, newspaper com-mentary in Israel suggests that there are sound strategic reasons for Israel to pursue such an option.[35]

The Need to Tighten the MTCR

The number of global suppliers of highly advanced LACMs has grown dramatically in the last decade. It is also clear – most prominently from the British and French decision to sell the *Black Shaheen* to the UAE – that the ground rules for handling cruise-missile transfers are dangerously ambiguous. Of special concern is the prospect that Russia and China will decide to exploit the confusion surrounding those ground rules and export highly advanced cruise missiles to potentially provocative states. Unless the MTCR's members achieve materially greater clarity and consensus on cruise-missile exports than exists today, the direct purchase of advanced LACMs from large industrial states may become a major source of cruise-missile proliferation.

Chapter 3

Motivations and Constraints Affecting the Pace and Scope of Proliferation

Technological skill, adequate foreign assistance, or easy opportunities to purchase complete systems from major suppliers represent only one side of the complex web of factors that are likely to shape the pace and scope of cruise-missile proliferation. All too frequently proliferation is seen as a product of raw technological determinism. The truth, though, is usually much more complex.

Any decision to acquire a major weapon system must be examined in the context of the acquiring state's process, however formal or informal, for developing military forces. Technological change affects the way military planners view future methods of warfare, as do the underlying doctrinal preferences of military institutions. These factors typically drive and constrain each other in interdependent ways. Also important are perceptions of a nation's regional and global adversaries. A given state may be less concerned with challenging intervention by the major powers than with countering long-standing regional threats that pose enduring and possibly unique military requirements. In any case, a regional state considering the acquisition of LACMs will factor into its decision both the challenges presented by adversary strengths and the opportunities implied by adversary weaknesses. Finally, the decision to expend major resources and to assimilate new weapon systems into a pre-existing force structure often occurs in a Byzantine bureaucratic setting involving inter-service and civilian–military rivalries.

These factors are sometimes facilitating and at other times constraining, and how they interact in a particular national context varies from country to country and may change over time. Although a comprehensive assessment is not practical here, it is illuminating to examine several broad categories of motivations and constraints pertaining to both cruise- and ballistic-missile acquisition.

Motivations to Acquire Missiles

Comparing ballistic- and cruise-missile choices has merit for several reasons, even though most states are likely eventually to acquire both types of missiles. The competing priorities are mainly a function of prestige, military utility and perceived adversary vulnerability.

Prestige

Prestige of ownership is frequently cited as a major factor explaining the attractiveness of acquiring ballistic missiles in the developing world.[1] Certainly, future adversaries of the US and its allies learned a key lesson from *Operation Desert Storm*: despite the coalition's punishing attacks on Iraqi forces, Iraq's ballistic missiles still posed a threat right up to the end of the conflict. Had Iraq struck earlier during the introductory phase of the intervention, had it possessed a nuclear weapon or used chemical or biological payloads, the outcome might well have been different. As it was, Iraq's crudely modified *Scuds* nearly managed to bring Israel into the war and drew off nearly 20% of the US F-15E air sorties to address the so-called '*Scud* hunt'.[2] Not only did Iraq's few allies crow over the merits of possessing ballistic missiles, it also seems clear that the war prompted a noticeable bump in ballistic-missile proliferation in the years immediately afterwards.[3]

The decisive role played by US *Tomahawk* cruise missiles in the Gulf War's air campaign greatly improved the prestige value of cruise missiles as well. This prestige seemed to be based not just on mere possession but also on the weapon's ability to deliver conventional payloads with great precision.[4] The fact that the *Tomahawk* has become the US weapon of choice for punishing violations of international norms may also have elevated the status associated with cruise-missile ownership.

The cruise missile's promise of precision delivery of conventional payloads may well provide a strong motivation for regional countries to acquire such delivery systems. Yet the threat posed by the capability to deliver WMD to increasingly long ranges remains a potent motivating factor for several states. Iran, North Korea, Iraq, India and Pakistan, among others, have all striven to acquire long-range ballistic missiles to satisfy regional and, in some cases, intercontinental strike ambitions. The palpable existence of a tested and serially produced force of intercontinental-range ballistic missiles would arguably convey more prestige and a stronger deterrent than the possession of regional-range cruise missiles or an indeterminate number of ship-borne cruise missiles earmarked for covert delivery.

Military Effectiveness

If a regional power were motivated simply by the need to possess missiles in order to threaten or coerce regional foes, or a US-led coalition, with crude terror attacks on cities using conventional warheads (or, alternatively, with chemical, biological or nuclear weapons), then relatively inaccurate ballistic missiles would probably suffice. A regional power, of course, would likely calculate such sufficiency by reference to the kinds of counter-force, active and passive measures that could be brought to bear to thwart such coercive objectives. If WMD threats are to play a featured role against a US-led coalition, though, then fear of retaliation – including the implicit threat of nuclear response – must also figure in a regional power's calculations. Despite Iraq's possession of ballistic missiles armed with chemical and biological warheads, the Western coalition apparently employed the threat of retaliation well enough to deter Saddam Hussein from crossing the WMD threshold.[5] No such fear prevented Iraq from using conventionally armed missiles, which, however inaccurate, still engendered apprehension about holding the coalition together and diverted a meaningful percentage of air sorties to forestall such a political outcome.

A critical issue shaping the pace and scope of cruise-missile proliferation is how far developing nations will be driven to acquire precision-attack delivery means. Conceivably, accurately delivered cruise missiles could provide strategic leverage, not only through

WMD coercion or use but also through conventional means. Satellite navigation is a far greater enabler of precision attacks for cruise missiles than it is for ballistic missiles. A cruise missile using only an INS system with a gyro drift rate of one degree per hour would achieve a CEP of over 1km at a range of 300km, and 4km at 600km.[6] Adding satellite navigation would transform it into a delivery system that could achieve a CEP of around 20m no matter what the range.[7] For a number of reasons, adding satellite navigation will have a far less substantial impact on the lethality of ballistic-missile attacks using conventional payloads. Because they are based on relatively primitive *Scud* missile technology, most ballistic missiles in developing-world inventories have CEP accuracies of between 1 and 2km.[8] Without sophisticated and costly manoeuvring re-entry vehicles or post-boost vehicles, these missiles can only make use of satellite navigation corrections until main engine cut-off, which occurs early in their flight sequence, and so can expect to improve their accuracy by around 20% at best.[9] Advanced short-range ballistic missiles that incorporate the ability to deploy a separating payload accurately can expect CEP improvements of about 70%.[10] Further improvements are conceivable, but these require extra-ordinarily sophisticated technology, such as the map-matching guidance schemes used in the US *Pershing* 2 missile. Such improvements are within the reach of a country like China, but ballistic-missile upgrades are difficult and expensive, and the relative ease and cheapness of greatly improving cruise-missile accuracy makes this route a more attractive one.

Besides precision delivery, LACMs also have several other operational advantages compared with ballistic missiles. Cruise missiles can be placed in canisters, which makes them especially easy to maintain and operate for extended periods in harsh environments. Even the unusually large *Silkworm*, just over 7m in length, could comfortably fit into a standard 12m shipping container, millions of which are carried each year into US ports. In contrast to larger ballistic missiles,[11] more modern and compact cruise missiles offer more flexible launch options (air, sea and ground), greater mobility for ground-launched versions and a smaller logistics burden, which could improve their pre-launch survivability. Moreover, cruise missiles need no special preparations to ensure launch-pad stability, which means that they can readily practice shoot-and-scoot tactics. And, because the small rocket motors that propel ground-launched cruise missiles off their launchers are not detectable by space-warning systems, cruise missiles will generally be less susceptible to post-launch counter-force attacks than ballistic missiles, which have readily detectable launch signatures.

Exploiting Adversary Vulnerability

Post-Gulf-War assessments of coalition vulnerabilities by foreign and coalition observers alike agree that Iraq failed abjectly to make the kind of careful assessment of coalition vulnerability that might have prompted even relatively ineffective attacks on coalition forces as they first arrived in Saudi Arabia.[12] The early build-up phase of any intervention is the most vulnerable period for several reasons. Command, control, communications and intelligence (C[3]I) systems are at their least effective early on, as it takes time to establish links between and among various service entities and coalition partners. Logistical nodes, consisting of sea ports and airfields of disembarkation, are a confused maze of operational activity early in a deployment. Most important, defences against missile attack are not always in place. One *Patriot* battalion of 96 missiles requires approximately 16 C-5 aircraft to deploy it into any theatre of operations.[13] Subjecting air bases to saturation missile attacks during this early phase will very likely overwhelm pre-existing defences and permanently incapacitate future ones.

Several disturbing trends combine to make modern aircraft extremely vulnerable to missile attacks. The first is the rising cost and complexity of high-performance aircraft. The cost means that smaller numbers of aircraft are procured, and the complexity encourages their concentration on a small number of air bases, along with specialised maintenance and repair facilities – as was evident during the Cold War in Central Europe, the Gulf War and NATO's Kosovo air campaign. This concentration, and consequent vulnerability to attack, has increased since the end of the Cold War, owing to the declining use of contingency airfields and hardened shelters for aircraft.[14] Furthermore, sortie generation from an air base requires a supporting infrastructure to prepare, launch, control, recover, rearm, refuel and maintain aircraft. Given the increasingly brittle nature of aircraft structures and materials, even modest levels of damage could achieve disproportionate debilitation.

Two Illustrative Scenarios

The vulnerability of air bases to precision attacks is best illustrated by considering two scenarios: one, a RAND Corporation assessment positing an Iranian attack by GPS-aided ballistic and cruise missiles on US Air Force aircraft bedded down at four air bases in Saudi Arabia; the other, a Chinese cruise- and ballistic-missile attack on four Taiwanese air bases prior to a large-scale cross-strait invasion. The first is set in 2007 and the second in 2010.[15]

Scenario 1

In the first scenario, Iran exploits a succession crisis and related civil war in Iraq in order to invade southern Iraq, to which the US responds in several ways, most prominently by deploying US aircraft to four Gulf air bases: Dhahran, Doha, Riyadh Military and Al Kharj. These bases have been used in the past for US aircraft deployments and are all within a missile threat range arc of just over 1,100km, as are other potential bases for deployment in Saudi Arabia and other Gulf states. Basing US short-range aircraft outside this range arc would greatly increase the number of tanker sorties required for in-flight refuelling. The four air bases used in this scenario together provide enormous ramp space for bedding down and supporting incoming aircraft: 14 parking areas totalling around 13.5m sq. ft, or nearly 1,000 football fields. Iran's strategy is to allow US aircraft to deploy within range of its cruise and ballistic missiles and to begin airlift operations. It would then conduct a coordinated cruise and ballistic-missile attack on these four air bases, using only conventional munitions.

In addition to GPS-aided missile guidance, the use of small submunitions drives the potential success of such coordinated attack. The effectiveness of submunitions compared to unitary warheads of the same weight is dramatic for soft targets like aircraft parked in the open. Against such a soft target, RAND calculations suggest that the lethal area of a small cruise missile with a 34kg payload (consisting of 1lb submunitions) is roughly three times greater using a submunition payload than using a unitary one. As payload increases so does the relative advantage of using submunitions. Thus, a 500kg M-9 ballistic-missile warhead would cover nearly eight times the area with submunitions compared with a unitary payload.[16]

Using just under 100 missiles altogether, the Iranian attack could achieve a 90% probability of kill against all aircraft on the parking ramps at four bases. The attack would consist of 60 GPS-guided ballistic missiles (30 M-9 and 30 M-18), along with 38 GPS-guided cruise missiles (converted unarmed UAVs with reciprocating engines cruising at sufficiently slow speeds to fly under the radar umbrella).[17] Attacking the large tent cities housing support personnel at each of the four bases, together with each base's missile-defence radar, would require an additional 40 ballistic missiles and 8 cruise missiles.

The limited role of cruise missiles in this scenario reflects the kind of cruise missiles selected for evaluation. One of the objectives of the exercise was to demonstrate how potential adversaries could exploit commercial and military technology to modify conventionally armed cruise and ballistic missiles to achieve a significant impact on air operations. The two unarmed UAVs chosen for analysis both had very modest payloads, and this dictated the limited role of cruise missiles.[18] Had modified kit aircraft been chosen instead, these slow-flying vehicles could have flown to roughly the same range with substantially larger payloads (some 150kg) at a quarter to a sixth of the cost.[19] Cruise missiles could have played an even more substantial role if, say, Russian or Chinese missiles had been part of the attack mix. Not only would their ranges and payloads be more comparable to M-9 and M-18 ballistic missiles, their flight speed would make coordinating their time of arrival with that of the ballistic missiles easier (eight- to nine-hour flights had to be assumed for the slow-flying UAVs). Closely timed cruise- and ballistic-missile attacks would severely tax ground-based radars supporting air defences.[20]

While the impact of such attacks would have a devastating effect on sortie generation, the political consequences of even modestly effective missile strikes might also be significant. Lt-Gen. Charles Horner, commander of US Central Command Air Forces during *Operation Desert Storm*, speaking a day after the Iraqi Scud attacks began on the night of 20 January 1991 said, 'Last night could have been the turning-point of the war. If he [Saddam Hussein] had hit Riyadh air base and destroyed six AWACS or put chemicals on the F-15s at Dhahran, think of how the attitude and support of the American people might have changed.'[21] The loss of so many critically important airborne warning and control system (AWACS) aircraft would also have had a palpable effect on the waging (if not the ultimate outcome) of the air campaign. Even worse, had Iraq possessed LACMs, the loss of six AWACS planes would have greatly affected the coalition's capacity to detect and destroy such missiles, because this depends heavily on AWACS warning and battle management capabilities. Finally, had Iraq been able to deliver chemical payloads, not only would allied sortie generation have diminished, but key US allies might have changed their minds about permitting access to critical air bases.

Thus, the particular appeal of LACMs turns both on their capacity to threaten without resorting to WMD use and on their implicit effectiveness for delivering WMD payloads. As noted earlier, the lethal area for a given quantity of biological or chemical agent delivered by a cruise missile can be at least ten times greater than that delivered by a ballistic missile.[22] In the hypothetical Iranian attack on four Gulf air bases, if chemical or biological payloads were employed, the effects would probably be even more devastating than the conventional attacks.[23] According to one study, air operations at 11 air bases in the region could be severely degraded (shutting down 80% or more of the air sorties) by the delivery of only 500 to 2,000kg of chemical agent (Sarin or VX), if delivered by missiles or aircraft.[24] Iran is estimated to possess an inventory of 2,000 tons (or roughly 2m kg) of chemical agents. Much smaller amounts of biological agent would be needed: 5–10kg of anthrax could cover most of an air base, assuming a cruise missile's more accurate means of delivery.

Scenario 2

In the second scenario, failure to resolve Taiwan's political status *vis-à-vis* the People's Republic of China precipitates a surprise People's Liberation Army (PLA) combined-arms assault on key elements of Taiwan's military and civilian infrastructure. Although the combined nature of the coordinated attack features an array of disparate forces (including electronic and information warfare assets, special operations forces and offensive and defensive aircraft), conventionally armed cruise and ballistic missiles play a critically important role in enabling China promptly to attain air superiority. The rationale is that in 2010 Taiwan's air force remains decidedly better than China's in virtually every category of comparison. Thus, unless China can employ its comparative advantage in land-attack cruise and ballistic missiles to leverage the effectiveness of its inferior air force, there is little prospect of China forcing Taiwanese capitulation or succeeding in a cross-strait invasion.

In 1999 the US Department of Defense issued a report to the Congress on the military balance between China and Taiwan in which several shortcomings in Chinese invasion capabilities were noted.[25] Nevertheless, the Pentagon concluded that – barring third-party intervention – China would be likely to succeed in a cross-strait invasion by 2005.[26] At present China cannot orchestrate the integrated, joint operations required to mount the kind of complex, multi-faceted military campaign reflected in the 2010 scenario. But in the hypothetical situation, a decade of Chinese strategic modernisation greatly improves the PLA's joint-operations and command-and-control capabilities, particularly its ability to execute closely timed precision-missile and air attacks on Taiwan's small number of critical air bases.

Two factors are critical in convincing PLA planners to accept the military risks of an attack: confidence in their force of 650 ballistic missiles and 400 LACMs, all within range of Taiwan; and the concentration of Taiwan's principal air-defence and strike aircraft at three of eight critical air bases. Ever since the PLA threatened Taiwan with ballistic-missile salvoes off its coast in 1996, analysts have focused almost entirely on China's build-up and deployment of ballistic missiles (M-9, M-18 and M-11), which reached roughly 650 in early 2010. Under-appreciated was China's companion build-up of LACMs (HN-1, -2 and -3), deployed on ground-mobile launchers, aircraft and submarines, and all within easy reach of key Taiwanese targets. This combination of growing Chinese missile capability interacts sharply with the way in which Taiwan concentrates its primary aircraft at three of its eight major air bases.[27] Some hangers are hardened, and a small strategic aircraft reserve remains hidden in hardened mountain bunkers near Chiayi and Hualien.

Employing tactical surprise, PLA planners begin their attack by using 75 ground-launched HN-1 and -2 cruise missiles (90% of which are equipped with ten submunition packages of runway cratering munitions[28]) to launch leading-edge strikes on the three primary Taiwanese air bases and one other housing airborne surveillance aircraft. Another ten or so cruise missiles take out Taiwan's *Patriot* missile defence radars to improve the prospects for subsequent ballistic-missile strikes. There are two reasons for using cruise missiles to open the conflict. Taiwan is assumed to have a US-supplied PAVE PAWS phased-array warning system to detect ballistic-missile launches and provide precise warning of ballistic missiles intended for particular Taiwanese targets; but the system can not do the same against cruise missiles, whose launch plumes are a fraction of the intensity of those from ballistic missiles. Moreover, the HN-2's 1,500km range permits PLA planners to use circuitous flight paths, essentially allowing a full 360° of freedom to approach each target. Flying earth-hugging flight profiles into their targets, 16 cruise missiles are sufficient to provide a 90% probability of temporarily closing the main runways and parallel taxiways, thus 'pinning down' Taiwanese aircraft.[29] Minutes after the cruise-missile attacks, satellite-aided ballistic-missile strikes commence on other important air-base targets (munitions storage, maintenance and repair facilities), early-warning and air-defence radars, and tactical command and control links. These attacks are accompanied by heavy jamming and information warfare attacks aimed at paralysing Taiwan's military command-and-control apparatus.

By pinning down Taiwanese aircraft on their bases, leading-edge missile strikes greatly reduce the number of Taiwanese air-defence interceptors that enter air-penetration corridors to meet the first wave of Chinese air strikes. Moreover, PLA aircraft released from such leading-edge missions, including air-defence suppression attacks, can fly to their target sets (primarily air bases) using higher and longer routes and carrying heavier payloads. Although the missile attacks alone may not be sufficient to shut down Taiwan's air bases, they can allow China to achieve air superiority over Taiwan in spite of having an inferior air force. China could then be in a position to negate Taiwan's ground forces and undertake a successful amphibious invasion, or pressure Taiwan to capitulate to its political demands.

Constraints Affecting Missile Acquisition

However compelling LACMs might appear as raw military tools conveying potent deterrent and military war-fighting capabilities, there are several constraining factors that inevitably temper motivations for acquiring them. Among the most important are the financial costs, particularly compared with alternative means of delivering conventional or WMD payloads; the challenges of assimilating new weapons into existing force structures; the impact of international export controls; and the effectiveness of Western deterrence and defence strategies.

Cost Comparisons

One frequently cited US Army estimate suggests that a developing nation could acquire at least 100 cruise missiles for $50m. The same investment would buy only 15 tactical ballistic missiles and three transporter-erector-launchers (TELs).[30] The assumption of a unit cost of $500,000 for a cruise missile is not far-fetched;[31] unit costs for cruise missiles appear to be coming down dramatically, driven especially by the increasing use of commercial off-the-shelf components. The US *Tomahawk* cruise missile costs roughly $1,200,000 but the US Navy's new tactical *Tomahawk* is expected to cost half that. The US Air Force and US Navy are close to fielding a functionally similar Joint Air-to-Surface Stand-off Missile (JASSM) at a unit cost of no more than $700,000 and a desired cost of $400,000. Russian *Alfa* and Chinese *Silkworm* ASCMs reportedly cost between $250,000 and $300,000.[32] And kit aircraft, transformed into unmanned land-attack systems, conceivably would cost around $50,000 apiece – perhaps even less if produced in fairly large lots, of roughly 500 units.

As for ballistic-missile costs, what data are available suggest that the ubiquitous *Scud* runs in the neighbourhood of $500,000 to $1m per missile, while the Chinese M-9 is close to $2m per unit.[33] Moreover, the support equipment needed to effect movement, command and control, launch and resupply operations in the field adds considerably to the unit cost of the ballistic-missile inventory. The fact that cruise missiles can be launched from aircraft and naval vessels, as well as ground launchers, not only adds flexibility but reduces overall system costs. Moreover, cruise-missile TELs are generally cheaper than those for ballistic missiles, in that they only require a simple zero-length launcher and rocket booster for missile launch.

Much is made of the general rule that reusable tactical aircraft can carry seven times the payload of a cruise or ballistic missile. But when the expected rate of attrition is factored in, a different picture emerges. One recent study concludes that, so long as cruise-missile attrition is less than 80%, cruise missiles are more cost-effective than manned aircraft.[34] But, no matter how appealing they might be from the standpoint of cost and military effectiveness, cruise missiles still need a strong bureaucratic champion to compete favourably with high-performance aircraft. One need only look at nearly 20 years of US Air Force and US Navy foot-dragging over any solid commitment to procure cruise missiles and UAVs in militarily significant quantities.[35] Aircraft platforms still dominate not just Western procurement priorities but those of most developing nations. Despite the facts that Iran's average level of defence spending has dropped sharply since the mid-1980s, and that it faces major challenges in modernising and expanding its forces, it remains wedded to a strategy of acquiring WMD-armed ballistic missiles and enough aircraft, armour and air defences to face a weakened Iraq and threaten tanker traffic in the Gulf.[36]

Force Structure Assimilation

If large numbers of LACMs are procured primarily to provide improved conventional war-fighting capability, as opposed to WMD delivery, integrating such units into existing force structures will be demanding. This is because no matter how effective conventionally armed cruise missiles may be, they rarely if ever become capable of single-handedly achieving major military objectives. In the Iranian scenario, cruise-missile attacks had to be precisely coordinated with ballistic-missile strikes. The China–Taiwan scenario involved even more complicated timing of attacks, including not only cruise- and ballistic-missile coordination but missile and aircraft sequencing as well. Having the confidence to conduct such complex integrated operations must derive from a significant commitment to tactical and doctrinal development, training, and realistic exercising and rigorous mission planning.

Assimilating missile units that have only WMD delivery missions represents a far less demanding and time-consuming task, because much less integration is required. For example, before *Operation Desert Storm*, US targeting circles presumed that Iraqi ballistic-missile units would follow an operational pattern dictated by the training received from Iraq's Soviet patrons: each missile battalion would be integrated into the operational fire plans of Iraqi ground force units. Instead, Iraqi missile units operated entirely separately (physically and from a command and control standpoint) from any other units in order to maintain their survivability, which they managed quite successfully. Moreover, their sporadic missile launches were not coordinated with other conventional fire. This pattern is very likely to be the one followed by states operating WMD-armed missile units.

The Effectiveness of Export Controls

Originated in 1987 by the US and its Group of Seven (G-7) partners, today's 33-nation MTCR is a politically rather than legally binding agreement among member-states to restrict the proliferation of rockets, unmanned aerial vehicles and related technologies capable of carrying a payload of 500kg for at least 300km. In 1993 the regime's guidelines were expanded to include missile-delivery systems capable of carrying biological and chemical warheads regardless of payload.

The regime is much more effective in controlling ballistic than cruise missiles. Two primary reasons account for this disparity. First, there is a reasonably solid consensus among members for restricting ballistic missiles; the same does not yet hold for cruise missiles and other UAVs. Second, because the MTCR does not restrict manned-aircraft exports, there are systematic exemptions for all civilian and military aircraft, and these can be used to work around many of the regime's restrictions on UAVs. Until the MTCR's shortcomings in the way it currently controls cruise missiles are rectified, cruise missiles will remain easier to acquire than ballistic missiles.

The Effects of Deterrence and Defence Strategies

A threshold determinant of how aggressively developing countries seek cruise-missile capabilities is their willingness to depend on GPS and GLONASS. In theory, the US and Russia could shut down GPS and GLONASS at will – although, given the phenomenal growth in civilian (and US military) dependence on satellite navigation, this appears highly doubtful. Moreover, concern over this dependence will probably impel other states, and perhaps commercial entities, to deploy their own GPS-equivalent systems.[37] Although GPS receivers are vulnerable to jamming, coupling the GPS receiver to an INS system will substantially thwart jamming,[38] which would involve a graceful degradation of accuracy. But this is likely to have no effect on WMD payloads, and only a marginal effect on conventional payloads earmarked for large area targets. Furthermore, high-quality digital map products will eventually permit developing nations to build TERCOM-like guidance systems for intermediate and terminal guidance – all without depending on satellite navigational aid.

In theory, US nuclear deterrence strategy should significantly constrain adversary dependence on either ballistic- or cruise-missile delivery of WMD payloads, and perhaps motivate adversaries to prefer cruise to ballistic missiles for delivering conventional munitions less subject to retaliatory threats. Nonetheless, although the US nuclear deterrent is far from becoming purely existential in its makeup, there is growing concern that US nuclear forces are not receiving the care and attention they merit. While declaratory policy still emphasises the deterrent's continuing importance, there has been palpable erosion of nuclear expertise and long-range planning, particularly in the operational forces.[39] Moreover, some analysts question whether declaratory policy is sufficiently unambiguous in dealing with threatening retaliation against non-nuclear states brandishing biological or chemical threats.[40]

As the status of nuclear deterrence has declined, the view has gained currency that conventional weapons, particularly 'smart' ones, are more credible and flexible than nuclear weapons as instruments of deterrence and war fighting. Conventional defence or denial strategy presupposes the capability to project and protect one's own forces overseas, and then to destroy the enemy's forces, including their WMD capabilities. Defending against an adversary's ballistic- and cruise-missile attacks is not only critical to the success of any conventional denial strategy, but the extent of its effectiveness could very well restrain an adversary from investing heavily in either or both ballistic and cruise missiles. Thus, Western capabilities to find and destroy missile launchers, intercept already launched missiles and passively protect intended targets are likely to affect acquisition choices.

Shortcomings exist in all three areas of missile defence. The effectiveness of counter-force operations against mobile missiles has not improved greatly since the end of the Gulf War. LACMs will only complicate counter-force operations, since their launchers are generally much smaller and harder for airborne sensors to identify than ballistic-missile TELs. As for passive defences, the expeditionary nature of US Air Force operations gives rise to a disinclination to burden limited air-transport resources with deployable shelters, and the bases they would deploy into are not hardened against the effects of missile attacks. Finally, active missile defences against both cruise and ballistic missiles remain minimal. Although some of today's theatre air defences have substantial capability against large LACMs flying relatively high flight profiles, severe combat identification problems need to be overcome. Once cruise missiles fly low, or add stealthy features or employ endgame countermeasures, further difficulties arise.

Unless adversaries of the US and its allies are driven to acquire precision-attack cruise missiles for purely conventional purposes, they are unlikely to seriously entertain large-scale acquisition of cruise missiles until Western defences against ballistic missiles are far better than they are today. In spite of the funds invested in theatre ballistic-missile defences, disruptive political expectations, poor management and serious technical challenges beset current programmes. These problems have contributed to a string of programme delays. Between now and 2007 the ability to defend against ballistic missiles will rest upon two lower-tier systems (the *Patriot* PAC-3 and the US Navy's *Standard* missile) and whatever counter-force operations can muster. Cruise missiles may become an increasingly attractive option to potential adversaries once ballistic-missile defences are greatly improved. But that will not occur until the political, technical and programmatic challenges facing the US Army's Theater High-Altitude Area Defence (THAAD) and the US Navy's Theater-Wide Defence (NTW) systems are overcome.

Chapter 4

Defending Against Cruise Missiles

The US and its allies have invested huge resources in air defence, including ground and airborne surveillance, fighter-based AAMs and SAMs. However effective these investments may be in dealing with manned-aircraft threats, there are notable shortcomings today in defence against low-flying cruise missiles. These will become still more apparent as threat numbers increase and low-observable capabilities become a more prominent feature of the cruise-missile threat.

Cold War Legacies

Existing air defences against manned-aircraft threats alone account for a US investment in the neighbourhood of several hundred billion dollars. This investment primarily supports tactical forces engaged around the globe. Primary components include such notable systems as the US Air Force's AWACS, the US Navy's E-2C *Hawkeye* airborne surveillance system, the US Army's *Patriot* missile, the US Navy's *Aegis* SAM (*Standard* missile) and an array of manned interceptors armed with AAMs. Sensors must be linked to shooters, so each of the military services furnishes the necessary command and control to manage the air-defence battle. Although investment in tactical air defences is significant, only a handful of manned interceptors supported by ground-based radars now provide strategic air defence for the continental US.[1]

Conceptually, the key objective of theatre air defences has always been to create as large a surveillance and engagement zone –

or battlespace – as possible. The potential payoff of such a strategy is significant. The concept of layered defence in depth allows for multiple shots, including counter-force attacks against enemy air bases, missile launchers and supply depots before takeoff or launch – thus potentially reducing his launch or salvo rate. Long-range detection of threats is also valuable, because the resultant warning permits passive-defence measures – such as scrambling to protective shelters or donning chemical suits – to be employed more effectively.

Although such a defence-in-depth strategy remains relevant today, there are several Cold War legacies that inhibit a truly integrated strategy. One is the limited amount of connectivity between the military services in such critical areas as BMC^3 and combat identification (CID), which distinguishes friendly aircraft from enemy threats. The US Navy tends to focus on scenarios involving defence in depth to protect a carrier task force, while the US Air Force focuses on wide-area air defence, using counter-air assets against enemy aircraft on the ground and AWACS and interceptors as an outer layer of defences. A more relaxed approach to defence in depth has generally applied to protecting land targets. Thus, in order to conduct their air-defence missions, each of the services has developed and procured equipment and procedures – encompassing BMC^3 systems, data links, message formats and doctrine – that are unique, rather than common.

Nonetheless, however ineffective today's air defences might be against advanced unmanned aerodynamic threats, they do provide something to build upon. This stands in contrast to the case of ballistic missiles: there was no legacy of defending against these before *Patriot*'s introduction during *Operation Desert Storm* a decade ago – and indeed US allies (except Israel, with its *Arrow* theatre missile defence programme) are still not significantly involved in developing layered defences against ballistic missiles. In the air-defence case, though, the success of defences against both manned and (in the British case) unmanned airborne threats during the Second World War did facilitate the creation of significant air-defence capabilities during the Cold War (much of the work occurring in a coalition setting within NATO). This analogy shows that the most promising approaches to meeting the challenges presented by low-flying cruise missiles are rooted in the air-defence systems in existence today.

Current and Prospective Shortcomings in Cruise-Missile Defence

Cruise missiles present particular challenges to air defences for a variety of reasons. Compared with the primitive German V-1s that attacked Britain during the Second World War, modern cruise missiles fly at one-tenth the altitude and have radar cross-sections (RCS) one hundred times smaller.[2] Arriving in large numbers they can overwhelm defences, even if detected in time to enable engagement. These challenges create severe shortcomings in today's air defences.

Connectivity Weaknesses

The presumption is that today's air defences could cope rather well with highly observable and relatively high-flying cruise missiles. But weaknesses in the sensor networking of BMC[3] and CID systems and doctrines call into question any such notion. Consider how Iraq might have employed LACMs to play havoc with coalition air defences during *Operation Desert Storm*. Since the coalition had essentially eliminated Iraq's aircraft threat, allied air defences could train their radars on *Scud* missiles, and it was easier for the radars to detect such high-angle missile trajectories. But, if Iraq had used both cruise missiles and ballistic missiles, the need to distinguish between incoming coalition aircraft and incoming Iraqi cruise missiles would have severely tested allied air and missile defences. Thus, not only would a cruise-missile threat mean missile defences having to cope simultaneously with high- and low-angle missile threats, it would also create the strong possibility of friendly-fire casualties – notwithstanding Western air dominance over any conceivable regional adversary.

No longer will the Gulf War's highly restrictive rules of engagement – which essentially shut down missile defences against everything but ballistic missiles – prevail in future contingencies. This prospect should force both the US and its potential coalition partners to take serious steps to improve air-defence connectivity. Friendly-fire or air-fratricide problems are by no means insignificant: perhaps the most prominent recent example was the inadvertent shooting down by friendly aircraft of two US Army *Blackhawk* helicopters over northern Iraq in April 1994. Yet that rather uncomplicated air environment pales to insignificance compared to the kinds of simulated air campaigns (without restricted rules of engagement) typically examined in joint US military exercises. In such simulations friendly-fire air casualties are reported to be routinely far above acceptable levels of aircraft attrition.[3] As cruise missiles grow stealthier, fratricide problems will increase. Lower RCS values for cruise missiles mean air defences must react more swiftly to ambiguous friend-or-foe challenges, and this increases the danger of their getting it wrong.

Another key weakness in connectivity is that airborne surveillance platforms collect surveillance data (which can be used to direct friendly fighters), but they do not directly provide fire-control data to ground- or sea-based SAMs. For example, a *Patriot* fire battery does not see a combat picture that extends for hundreds of kilometres; its picture is constrained by the line-of-sight range to the horizon of its own associated radar: 25km or less. Fighters, too, are constrained, because airborne platforms currently cannot cue or supply fire-control information to their AAMs. Hence, SAMs and AAMs can only engage cruise missiles at relatively short ranges, which prevents in-depth layered defence. These limitations create enormous opportunity costs: wide-area defence against cruise missiles would soak up unacceptably large numbers of SAMs, AAMs and fighters needed for other crucial missions.

Performance Degradation of Air-defence Radars

The detectability of cruise missiles by radar is a function of their RCS value and how low they can fly. One example powerfully illustrates the impact of changes in RCS. An AWACS surveillance aircraft can detect an enemy aircraft with a $7m^2$ RCS travelling at 800km/hr at a distance of 370 km. This equates to roughly 28 minutes of time to react and engage the target. But a smaller cruise missile, with an RCS of $0.1m^2$, travelling at the same speed would be detected only at a range of about 130km, leaving only 10 minutes reaction time. Cruise missiles with an RCS of $0.0001m^2$ are conceivable in the near future. Assuming they fly at the same speed of 800km/hr, AWACS detection would occur (if at all) at less than 25km, leaving under two minutes in which to react to the threat (see Figure 1).[4]

Quite apart from the decreasing RCS values of small cruise missiles, low-level flight paths severely stress both airborne and ground-based radars. This is because terrain-hugging cruise missiles can literally hide in the competing background clutter of the earth's surface. Ground clutter is the mass of irrelevant radar signal returns produced by a vast range of things (people, vehicles, trees, mountains, valleys, birds, insects, etc.), and the challenge for radar is to process all this background and pull the faint cruise-missile signature out of it.[5] To make the processing easier, most US computer-controlled air-defence radars have been designed to ignore slow-moving objects on the ground – such as tanks, trucks and cars moving at speeds under about 80 knots. This creates the possibility of exploiting the clutter-rejection features of modern air defences by using slow- and low-flying converted kit planes and UAVs, as discussed in Chapter 2.

Many ground-based radars supporting today's air-defence missiles reduce the amount of ground clutter by tilting the search beam back about 3°, effectively lifting it above the ground. This increases the chances that a low-flying cruise missile will go undetected. Furthermore, whereas airborne radar systems can see several hundreds of kilometres, the earth's curvature means that ground-based *Patriot* and *Aegis* radars trying to detect a cruise missile flying at 50m altitude might first see it only when it has closed to some 35km or less.[6]

Figure 1 Radar Cross-Section

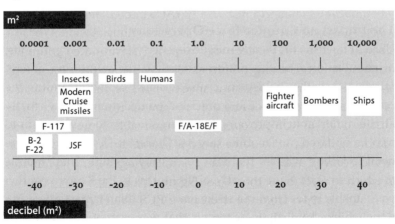

Sources Aviation Week & Space Technology, 5 February 2001; author's estimates

Finally, as RCS values of adversary cruise missiles plummet, adding endgame countermeasures (such as towed decoys or terrain-bounce jammers) to stealthy cruise missiles will tax existing missile sensors even more. Such countermeasures are highly synergistic with low-RCS missiles, because their effectiveness is enhanced if the signature they disguise is already insignificant.

The High Cost of Defence

Perhaps the most dramatic effect of the widespread proliferation of cheap cruise missiles would be to create unaffordable cost-exchange ratios for the defender. The increasing unit cost of the *Patriot* PAC-3 missile, for instance, may be so high that missile inventories must be kept to a minimum. Consequently, large raids or saturation attacks with cheap cruise missiles could easily draw critically valuable (and expensive) defences away from still more important missions, like defending against ballistic or stealthy cruise missiles. Costs will rise further if more sophisticated cruise missiles spread widely. Such spread will create the need for improvements in (and increased unit costs for) surface-to-air and air-to-air missile seekers, as well as for airborne sensors. One of several studies of the expected costs of defending against cruise missiles underscores the critical importance of seeking lower-cost alternatives;[7] it shows that effective defence against a salvo attack of 200 cruise missiles would require an investment of $475m, or $4m per kill. In such circumstances inventories would dwindle, and other missions would be compromised.

The Impact on Counter-force Operations

US joint doctrine for theatre missile defence views attack operations, or counter-force, as the preferred method for countering enemy missiles – whether ballistic or cruise missiles. Notwithstanding the revolution in surveillance and precision-guided munitions, virtually all the remarkable improvements in targeting up to now pertain to attacks on fixed, not mobile, targets. *Operation Desert Storm's* one notable failure was its inability to destroy a single Iraqi mobile missile launcher. More recently, NATO forces in the Kosovo conflict were unable to identify and strike moving Serbian targets operating under thick cloud cover, or targets that were camouflaged or well concealed.[8]

Ground-launched cruise missiles only make the counter-force problem more difficult. Pre-launch detection and attack is obviously preferable, especially if the missile carries a WMD warhead – but pre-launch detection of WMD-armed missiles will become more difficult as ground-launched cruise missiles proliferate. The proportion of civilian and military vehicles with essentially the same characteristics as missile launchers will more than double as smaller cruise-missile launchers are deployed, and as this 'look-alike', or 'confuser', population grows, airborne surveillance sensors will be hard pressed to distinguish real targets from false ones[9] (and hitting the wrong target not only wastes precious attack resources, it also frequently entails huge political costs). Moreover, post-launch detection will fare no better; cruise-missile launch signatures, unlike those for ballistic missiles, are too faint for space-based launch-detection satellites to register.

Improvements to counter-force operations against mobile missiles are feasible, but so far the Department of Defense has not matched its pro-counter-force rhetoric with either sufficient funding or disciplined management. Generally less than 5% of the Pentagon's overall missile-defence budget is allocated to counter-force improvements, and this is scattered among a poorly managed array of piecemeal programmes.[10]

Passive-defence Weaknesses

At the height of the Cold War, NATO air bases in Central Europe employed a variety of passive-defence measures to protect their aircraft from Warsaw Pact missile and air attacks. These included hardened aircraft shelters at main operating air bases, 'bare bases' (pre-positioned modular support components at dispersed operating airfields) and equipment and procedures for rapid runway repair and chemical decontamination to cope with conventional and chemical attacks. Unfortunately, aside from what can be brought in by air,[11] such passive-defence measures are not in place at most air bases to which US and coalition aircraft would now deploy in case of war. Some shelters do exist at air bases in South Korea and the Middle East, but the number of tactical aircraft expected to deploy there grossly exceeds available shelters. Moreover, the large size of critically important surveillance, targeting, refuelling and strategic lift aircraft makes protecting these aircraft prohibitively expensive.

Nor would hardened shelters or additional runways afford protection for support personnel or the supporting infrastructure required to maintain, recover, re-arm, re-fuel and direct sortie generation.

As illustrated in Chapter 3, the advent of precision-attack systems greatly exacerbates these passive-defence weaknesses. But – particularly in light of competing demands for defence resources – defence planners generally do not favour expending huge resources on fixed passive defences in several sites when only one might actually become a flash point.[12]

Hedging Against Cruise-missile Threats

Even though the politics and funding priorities of ballistic-missile defence capture most if not all the attention of both popular and specialist media, existing and prospective shortcomings in cruise-missile defences have not gone entirely unnoticed. In January 1995 the Pentagon's *Report of the Defense Science Board Summer Study Task Force on Cruise Missile Defense* drew critical attention to the problem. A year later another Defense Science Board revisited the question to check on progress made in light of the original recommendations.[13] The US Congress, too, entered the picture, when it fashioned the 'Cruise Missile Defense Initiative' in its *National Defense Authorization Act of Fiscal Year 1996*. The act stipulated that the Department of Defense should strengthen defences against existing and near-term threats, and also urged it to undertake a well coordinated technology development programme to support future deployment of effective defences against advanced cruise missiles.[14] The Pentagon seems to have taken the Congressional guidance to heart, as its own strategic planning document, the Defense Planning Guidance (DPG), states that capabilities are needed to defend against difficult-to-detect cruise missiles by 2010. Furthermore, the DPG charges the services to be positioned to respond to an even earlier emergence of the cruise-missile threat.[15]

Impediments to Progress

Despite official awareness of the problem, the US has made little significant progress in rectifying current and prospective shortcomings in cruise-missile defence.[16] Although in 1996 the

Pentagon fashioned a new organisation called the Joint Theater Air and Missile Defense Organization (JTAMDO), this is seen as a waste of Joint Staff resources and a threat to service prerogatives on theatre missile defence. Rumours of its imminent demise abound.[17] Despite rhetorical attention to joint solutions, each service continues to pursue its own vision of cruise-missile defence. But effective defences will not be possible until all the services possess better elevated sensors capable of providing longer-range surveillance and fire-control-quality information to AAMs and ground- and ship-based SAMs. The latter, too, require improved sensors to cope with lower-cross-section missiles and possible countermeasures. Piece-meal efforts will not add up to an effective wide-area defence against cruise missiles. Furthermore, coalition operations do not only require allies to improve their own weapon sensors, they demand US willingness, and allied capacity, to share distributed weapon-engagement information. Because the necessary investments in developing various technologies have not been made, it is now virtually impossible to meet the DPG's 2010 readiness goal.[18] Should significant threats emerge before 2010 the services are clearly even less prepared.

The absence of an agreed-upon threat has contributed to such dismal progress.[19] The expectation is that over time the cruise-missile threat will evolve in severity from relatively few and highly observable missiles in the near-term (1–5 years from now), via higher numbers of lower observable, terrain-hugging missiles in mid-term (5–15 years), to large numbers of stealthy missiles with countermeasures in the long-term (15+ years). Low RCS value and low-altitude flight are the primary technological determinants of air-defence improvements; hence, the preference is that such missiles emerge in the mid- to far-term future.[20] But if the MTCR is not strengthened, or if US–Russian and US–Chinese relations deteriorate, then it is conceivable that modest numbers of stealthy cruise missiles with endgame countermeasures – and perhaps larger numbers of cheap, slow-flying UAVs – could emerge five to ten years hence. Concerted diplomatic engagement is needed to prevent this occurring, or at least to control its damaging effects; appropriate investment in technology development is also needed to hedge against its unfolding.[21]

The divergence of service views about how the threat might unfold may be a convenient cover for deferring allocations for cruise-missile defences. The need to defend against difficult-to-detect cruise missiles also suggests entirely new operational concepts that threaten conservative military organisations. For example, broad-area-defence concepts might entail feeding fire-control decisions from an airborne platform controlled by one service to the ground- and sea-based SAMs of the other services. Inter-service tension may be natural, and even essential to achieving well-considered joint solutions, but arriving at appropriate hedging strategies will require strong direction from senior civilian and military leaders to keep nascent cruise-missile defences in line with evolving threat developments.[22]

Hedging Priorities

Assuming that most if not all of the current obstacles to progress can be mitigated, a fairly straightforward path to improving legacy air defences against the emerging cruise-missile threat is discernible. Meeting the technical challenges entails:

- implementing improved mechanisms for fighting jointly, including with coalition partners;
- restoring lost battlespace by improving sensor capabilities for detecting, tracking and intercepting low-RCS cruise missiles with endgame countermeasures;
- finding more affordable ways to defend against low-cost cruise-missile threats; and
- developing new approaches to locating and attacking cruise-missile launchers before missiles are launched.

Defending Jointly: Creating a Single Integrated Air Picture (SIAP)

Providing a common air picture with greatly improved capacity to distinguish friendly aircraft from enemy cruise missiles requires the merging of various service and Ballistic Missile Defense Organization (BMDO) BMC³ programmes to achieve interconnectivity among a disparate array of service sensors and shooters. This is a long-standing quest, begun formally in 1969 with programmes that aimed to improve tactical air control. However, the advent of fast, low-flying and (especially) low-observable cruise missiles magnifies the need to create true service interoperability. Simply put, SIAP would allow various sensor data sent via disparate service data links to be integrated to form (or display) a single view of the air picture, available to all relevant units in a given theatre.[23] Having one fully coordinated view of the air picture would accelerate decision-making on identifying friend from foe, prioritising weapon selection and executing air-defence engagements.

Creating a fully effective SIAP is impossible without US leadership in bringing key allies and friends into such an effort. Alliance mechanisms should be used to explore external interface standards for disparate data links. The biggest hurdle lies in the sensitivity of sharing data-link protocols and encryption with some allies and friends. However, much can be achieved through common interface standards and interface hardware to permit a necessary level of data-sharing about air threats. The benefits of such data-sharing clearly outweigh the risks. Indeed, the US would be better prepared to engage air threats in the critical early stage of a contingency, when it is least capable, if host-nation assets and coalition air defences were fully interoperable with US air-defence assets.

Despite the obvious and long-standing need for a SIAP capability, limited funding and a clear lack of progress have rendered efforts to achieve it inadequate.[24] At a news conference on 7 December 2000 Lt-Gen. John Costello, Chief of the US Army Space and Missile Defense Command, told reporters that 'the Army does not know what specifications will have to be met to make its air and missile defence systems interoperable with others throughout the military because the requirements for SIAP have yet to be defined'.[25] The latest push towards achieving a partial SIAP is a two-year joint task force effort, chartered in late 2000, to integrate the tracking and identification activities of the US Navy's *Aegis*, the US Army's *Patriot* and the US Air Force's AWACS.[26] However demanding the technical challenges, implementing SIAP appears to be more dependent on service commitment and appropriate funding levels. Both are urgently needed if any significant progress, particularly as to coalition operations, is to occur by the end of this decade.

Restoring Lost Battlespace

Improved connectivity through a SIAP capability represents a necessary, but not sufficient, solution to restoring the battlespace lost by virtue of terrain-hugging, low-RCS cruise missiles. The performance of airborne surveillance radars and missile seekers must also be improved. Most important, new surveillance and fire-control sensors must eventually be deployed on airborne platforms and linked to SAMs and AAMs to furnish wide-area defence.[27] Called air-directed surface-to-air missile (ADSAM), the concept would radically alter the current decentralised approach to fire control, whereby each SAM is guided to its target by its own ground-based, horizon-limited radar.[28] Instead, ADSAM entails placing a new surveillance and fire-control radar on an elevated platform capable of tracking stealthy cruise missiles out to hundreds of kilometres. This centralised fire-control platform could then direct a ground-based SAM by providing mid-course or terminal guidance updates, or the SAM could guide itself in the terminal phase with its own on-board seeker. The key point is that, because it is airborne, ADSAM enables ground-based SAMs to intercept targets to their full potential range (100–150km), unhampered by the 25–35km limit imposed by their horizon-limited ground-based radars. Besides fire control for air-directed SAMs, such an elevated platform could also furnish precision cues to fighter weapons to increase the effectiveness of AAMs to their full potential range (around 60km).

The benefits flowing from ADSAM are numerous. Most valuable is the significant increase in the depth of fire for all weapon systems, which creates multiple-shot opportunities and greatly reduced leakage against large onslaughts of cruise missiles. The possibility of fratricide would also be greatly reduced, owing to the availability of high-quality fire-control information on targets identified and tracked over great distances. Moreover, under the ADSAM concept a single SAM battery could (depending on the particular system) provide defence for 10,000–70,000km^2 of territory; this would relax the need to bunch SAM batteries around point targets to provide 360° protection against cruise missiles. Less reliance on ground-based radars could streamline the process of deploying into regional campaigns, make more efficient use of already limited SAM inventories and provide force protection early in any regional campaign, when defences are least capable. Finally, a long-range airborne surveillance and fire-control radar could conceivably contribute to ballistic-missile defence by providing launch-related cues to a fighter-based boost-phase defence system.[29]

Despite these virtues, the expense of developing and procuring a new airborne surveillance and fire-control system has inhibited the US Air Force from aggressively pursuing full implementation in a fixed-wing aircraft. The E-3 AWACS or, more likely, the E-8 Joint Surveillance Target Attack Radar System (JSTARS) are conceivable platforms.[30] Reportedly, as part of its Radar Technology Insertion Program (RTIP) for JSTARS, the US Air Force has under development improvements that would incorporate advances in radar technology that would double the E-8's acuity and allow tracking of fast, stealthy cruise missiles at hundreds of kilometres. But RTIP reportedly has been put on mere 'life support' in the 2002–2007 budget cycle, most likely due to the significant rise in funding (roughly $100m per year) needed to implement the ADSAM concept in JSTARS.[31]

A near-term, though lesser performing, alternative to a fixed-wing surveillance and fire-control solution is the US Army's Joint Land-attack Cruise Missile Defense Elevated Netted Sensor System (JLENS). In late 1995 the US Army was designated the lead service to develop a jointly used surveillance and fire-control sensor suite deployed on aerostat platforms (blimp-like balloons, using lighter-than-air gas for buoyancy).[32] JLENS would be weather-limited and take time to deploy in distant regional contingencies; also, flying at 10,000–15,000ft, it would have far greater problems with terrain masking than JSTARS flying some two-and-a-half times higher.[33] Nonetheless, it could complement faster-reacting, weather-insensitive, more mobile fixed-wing aircraft. Its special appeal as a complementary system is its ability to stay on station for an extremely long time during lengthy pre-hostility periods, or during peacekeeping operations, for one-tenth the cost of a fixed-wing aircraft.[34]

Besides restoring battlespace through improved elevated sensors, other parts of the air-defence kill chain will need improvements as well. To cope with high-clutter environments and increasingly stealthy cruise missiles employing endgame counter-measures, upgrades to seekers for air-to-air and surface-to-air missiles are needed. So far, the services have shown uneven progress. The US Air Force is out in front but exclusively focused on a fighter-based solution. The US Army's JLENS programme lacks the necessary performance and is 'joint' in name only, with the other services showing scant interest. And if failure to invest in upgrading its *Standard* missile and E2-C *Hawkeye* surveillance aircraft is any indication, the US Navy would seem to have higher priorities than full participation in a joint theatre air-defence system.[35] Several billion dollars of unplanned investments may account for service reticence, but unless the uneven service progress is corrected, it will doom any effort to bring about truly integrated, joint air defence against cruise missiles within the next decade.

Making Air Defence Affordable

The cost-per-kill arithmetic of cruise-missile defence is stark: whether a *Patriot* PAC-3 air-defence missile costs $5m or less than half that, the figure compares most unfavourably with a $50,000 unmanned kit aircraft. Clearly, Western defence planners must work towards finding more affordable solutions to defending against large raids of cheap UAVs and kit aircraft.

Simple, cheap solutions permitting defence against conventionally armed and slow-flying UAVs or kit aircraft are conceivable. Passive-defence measures suitable for protecting air bases are quite expensive, and most dictate infrastructure commitments requiring the military to know where it will fight next.[36] On the other hand, short-term active defences to protect an air base might prove more feasible. Small machine-gun teams or radar-guided guns could be employed around the base's perimeter,[37] and night-vision goggles could be used to detect, track and engage slow-flying targets that had managed to evade airborne air defences. But these devices would not allow target acquisition at ranges beyond about 500m. If UAVs or kit aircraft (or, for that matter, GPS-guided cruise missiles) carried biological or chemical agents, and if the intended targets were not just air bases but cities or other large area targets, then broad area coverage and as much battlespace as possible would be needed to allow multiple shots – a mere 500m would not be enough.[38] Engaging slow-fliers further out would require modification of existing systems, such as AWACS, JSTARS and *Patriot*, to permit them to track targets in the 60–90-knot range, and JSTARS would be best suited to handle the task of passing acquired precision tracking information to defensive missiles for engagement.[39] Even so, unless the cost of defensive interceptors can be driven down dramatically, the offence still could threaten to exhaust the defensive missile inventories.

Securing defence system affordability lies primarily in finding ways to drive down the high cost of missile seekers. The Pentagon's Defense Advanced Research Projects Agency (DARPA) has invested modestly in approaches that exploit the latest technologies to provide significant savings in seeker costs, using commercial parts to the maximum extent practical and trading some performance for cost.[40] Provided the ADSAM concept is implemented, though, some trade-off is permissible. Precision fire-control information furnished to a low-cost interceptor could guide it into a narrow basket, whereupon its on-board seeker would engage the incoming missile. A variety of different air-, sea- or ground-based platforms could be modified to launch such low-cost interceptors.[41]

Making Counter-force Feasible

Improving counter-force targeting against mobile missile launchers depends not so much on increased resources as on senior Pentagon leadership commitment to radical experimentation, new operational concepts and organisational change. Military planners must acknowledge that WMD-armed mobile missiles, ballistic and cruise alike, are not 'just another target'.[42] Tracking them effectively merits the same dedicated round-the-clock treatment that the US Navy has devoted to tracking enemy submarines. This calls for original thinking about how to mesh the intelligence-gathering and operational-targeting duties of the several services into a single joint entity charged with tracking and targeting such high-priority threats.[43] Because existing airborne surveillance systems like JSTARS cannot operate freely over denied areas, a breakthrough in space-based observation seems essential. One new idea, *Discoverer II*, would depart from the standard government practice of procuring essentially hand-built, expensive single-satellite systems. Instead it would exploit commercial manufacturing practices to deploy a constellation of 24 or more radar satellites in low-earth orbit, or enough to provide nearly continuous tracking of moving objects on the ground.[44] Without such radical departures from standard Pentagon practices, there is little hope of achieving more than marginal improvements in finding and attacking mobile missiles.[45]

Enter Homeland Defence

Several features of cruise missiles, not least their compact size and ease of maintenance, have suggested to some analysts that they may become an attractive alternative for states or terrorist groups lacking the resources or technical skills to build and deploy intercontinental-range ballistic missiles. In this context, the covert deployment of an LACM on a commercial vessel represents the scenario of greatest concern.[46] There are thousands of commercial container ships in the international fleet, and US ports alone handle over 13m containers annually. Even a large, bulky cruise missile like the Chinese *Silkworm* could readily fit into a standard 12m shipping container equipped with a small internal erector for launching.[47] Such a ship-launched cruise missile could be positioned just outside territorial waters to strike virtually any important capital or large industrial area anywhere on the globe. And, because a cruise missile is an ideal means for efficiently delivering small but highly lethal quantities of biological agent, a state or terrorist group could forego acquiring or building a nuclear weapon without sacrificing the ability to cause catastrophic damage.

All the weaknesses in defending against cruise missiles in theatre campaigns are compounded by the challenges of homeland defence. The US-Canadian North American Air Defense Command (NORAD) routinely detects and tracks ballistic-missile threats to North America. Ideally, doing the same for cruise-missile launches using space-based sensors would be a good starting point. But, according to one conservative estimate, it will take at least another three decades before space-based sensors might become capable of reliably detecting and tracking low-flying cruise missiles.[48] This means that NORAD must rely on airborne surveillance platforms for the foreseeable future – a daunting task, given the expanse of territory it must monitor. In peacetime, however, relying on airborne surveillance around the clock is simply too expensive. In wartime NORAD could currently muster fighter aircraft to respond to small numbers of cruise-missile threats, but to launch airborne surveillance aircraft it must rely on strategic warning information. Expectations about acquiring such warning of attack differ between wartime and peacetime. During the 1990–91 Gulf War, the US inter-agency counter-terrorism organisation, operating on heightened alert and interacting with friendly governments, pre-empted around 40 terrorist attempts aimed at US-related targets at home or abroad.[49] Yet various successful terrorist acts since the end of the Gulf War point to the difficulty of confidently providing strategic warning of attack except in war conditions.

Finally, the organisational shortcomings that hamper progress in cruise-missile defences for regional campaigns also beset routine planning for homeland defence against cruise missiles. No single service or agency, such as the BMDO for ballistic-missile defence, is mandated to address such normal bureaucratic routines as establishing requirements and technology planning. Moreover, any prospective solution necessarily must involve both US and Canadian military services, law enforcement agencies and intelligence organisations.[50]

Any effort to construct a homeland defence against cruise missiles would hinge on acquiring warning-of-attack information with a minimum of false alarms and on exploiting progress made in theatre air defences against cruise missiles.[51] A significant challenge is monitoring ships embarking from ports of concern around the globe. A large constellation of space-based satellites, as contemplated in *Discoverer II*, would be needed to satisfy such a huge monitoring requirement. The national defence kill chain would not be qualitatively unlike that for theatre air defence, but much larger in scale and much more expensive. Particularly critical is progress on airborne surveillance and precision fire control. NORAD is currently seeking funding to investigate the potential utility of a stratospheric airship.[52] Essentially a solar-powered, untethered, radar-equipped balloon, the airship would fly at 70,000ft to provide surveillance and target identification of low-flying cruise missiles, presumably to air-, sea- and ship-based interceptors. Some savings might be achieved by basing such interceptors on unmanned combat aerial vehicles (UCAVs) rather than manned aircraft. But, no matter what benefits may accrue from exploiting new approaches to cruise-missile defence, it seems reasonable to predict, however crudely, that any limited defence of the entire US homeland against cruise missiles would cost at least $30–40bn, or roughly half the Clinton administration's proposed budget for national ballistic-missile defence.[53]

Given that reducing the ballistic-missile threat will mean raising the cruise-missile threat, the US Department of Defense should investigate homeland protection against cruise missiles as well. Two study groups of government and industry specialists have already evaluated the question. The first, directed on the basis of language in the 1997 Quadrennial Defense Review, met in 1998 and laid the groundwork for a subsequent, more rigorous evaluation during 2000 of potential architectures and related costs for a cohesive system to improve national cruise-missile defence.[54]

Chapter 5

Strengthening Non-proliferation Policy

Effective controls on the spread of cruise missiles and related technologies would not only improve the predictability of the threat and slow its emergence, it would also greatly reduce the cost of missile defences. Yet among most advocates of missile defence and many die-hard arms controllers the consensus is emerging that curbing cruise-missile proliferation is a lost cause. The former naturally see rapid deployment of missile defences as the only prescription for its consequences, while the latter search pessimistically for stronger and legally binding international norms in the form of a new treaty.[1] Like so many complex national security issues, however, the prescription calls for a modest dose of each nostrum. On the one hand, more effective hedging strategies to cope with the threat's possible emergence would not only serve US defence objectives better, they might make prospective adversaries less inclined to invest in cruise missiles. On the other hand, addressing current weaknesses in the MTCR's rules on the transfer of both complete systems and dual-use technologies might inhibit the worst manifestations of the threat for significant time periods. Both would present defence planners with a more orderly and predictable threat evolution and render them much less liable to surprise.

Despite its shortcomings, the MTCR has arguably brought a significant degree of order and predictability to containing the spread of ballistic missiles. Most missile programmes that raise concerns today have their origin in the widely proliferated *Scud* missile, essentially a 1950s Soviet improvement on the Nazi V-2 missile.[2] The poor accuracy, clumsy logistics, limited payload and other weaknesses of the *Scud* and its many derivatives inhibit their users' capacity to create flexible and confident attack options that go beyond the crude delivery of WMD. Their poor performance also makes them easier to defend against than ballistic missiles with TERCOM guidance systems, manoeuvrable re-entry vehicles and solid-rocket motors. With the Soviet Union no longer dispensing *Scuds* to its client states, North Korea is left as the main supplier of MTCR-restricted ballistic missiles.[3]

Further, many of the MTCR's most notable but more mundane successes in denying the export of dual-use components listed in the regime's technical annex have gone largely unnoticed.[4]

Notwithstanding the prevailing scepticism, there is scope for building on the MTCR to create effective impediments to cruise-missile proliferation. Understanding the MTCR's weaknesses is the essential first step in considering a menu of improvements. At the same time, the persistent calls to reinvent the MTCR by transforming it into a legally binding international treaty deserve examination, if only to refine the proper focus of future efforts.

An MTCR Primer

The MTCR is the only existing multilateral arrangement covering the transfer of missiles and related equipment, material and technology relevant to WMD delivery. Its purpose is to seek member adherence to an agreed set of export-policy guidelines. These guidelines are applied to an extensive list of items contained in the regime's equipment and technology annex (as Figure 2 shows, this is divided into two categories of controlled items). The MTCR's general guidance directs members to make a 'strong presumption to deny' transfers of any annex item or any missile (whether or not MTCR-restricted) that the member believes is intended for the delivery of WMD warheads. Member-states are obligated to make an assessment of the recipient state's missile and space programmes and determine the extent to which the transfer contributes to the development of delivery systems (other than manned aircraft) for WMD payloads.[5]

Category I

To all intents and purposes, Category I items – the most stringently

Figure 2 The Missile Technology Control Regime

Members as of June 2001
South Korea joined the MTCR in March 2001, bringing membership to 33 states.

Argentina
Australia
Austria
Belgium
Brazil
Canada
Czech Republic
Denmark
Finland
France
Germany
Greece
Hungary
Iceland
Ireland
Italy
Japan
Luxembourg
Netherlands
New Zealand
Norway
Poland
Portugal
Russia
South Africa
South Korea
Spain
Sweden
Switzerland
Turkey
Ukraine
UK
US

Overview The Missile Technology Control Regime (MTCR) was established in 1987 by the US and its Group of Seven (G-7) partners – Canada, France, Germany, Italy, Japan and the United Kingdom. There are currently 33 member-states and several 'adherents', including Israel and, more ambiguously, China. The MTCR seeks to limit the proliferation of rockets, unmanned aerial vehicles and related technologies capable of carrying a payload of 500 kilogrammes for at least 300 kilometres. In 1993, the guidelines were extended to include missile-delivery systems capable of carrying biological and chemical warheads. The Regime is politically binding only and not part of a legal treaty regime. The members unilaterally implement the agreed export control standards.

Categories
Category 1 300km range, 500kg payload
Category 1 items – consisting of complete systems, major sub-systems and their technology and production facilities – are most sensitive. The MTCR specifies that member-states will practice a particular restraint in consideration of Category 1 transfers regardless of their purpose, and that there is a strong presumption to deny such transfers. The same presumption of denial applies to systems of any range and payload and to any other item on the MTCR control list if there is persuasive evidence that they are intended to be used to deliver weapons of mass destruction (WMD).
Category 2 300km range, regardless of payload
Category 2 items consist of complete sub-Category 1 systems capable of a range of 300km with any payload, as well as a long list of dual-use components. The MTCR specifies that Category 2 items must be subjected to a case-by-case export review and will require government-to-government end-use and end-user assurances if they could contribute to the delivery of WMD.

Sources http://www.state.gov/www/global/arms/np/ mtcr/mtcr.html; *The Military Balance 1997/98* (Oxford: Oxford University Press for the IISS, 1997), pp. 290–91.

controlled – are automatically considered able to 'contribute' to the development of WMD-armed missiles.

Item 1 of the category includes complete rocket systems (including ballistic missiles, space-launch vehicles and sounding rockets) and UAVs (including cruise missiles, target drones and reconnaissance drones) capable of delivering 500kg payloads (the weight of a relatively crude nuclear weapon) to a range of 300km (the strategic range in the most compact theatres where nuclear weapons might be used) or more.

Item 2 includes certain major subsystems usable in rockets and UAVs that meet the 300km/500kg threshold, as well as specially designed production equipment for these missiles and their major subsystems.

A critically important change to the Category I guidelines was made in 1993, when language was added directing members to assess whether recipient states could modify missiles or components via range/payload trade-offs so as to develop missiles meeting the 300km/500kg threshold. Although it applies to both ballistic and cruise missiles, this addition is particularly important in light of the ease of customising highly modular cruise missiles.

Because Category I items are inherently usable as – or in the development of – missiles for WMD delivery, MTCR members are admonished to make a 'strong presumption to deny' their transfer, regardless of the recipient's intended end use. In the unlikely case that a member-government decides to export a Category I item, it must obtain binding government-to-government assurances and take all precautions necessary to ensure that the item is not diverted to a WMD delivery system.

Category II

MTCR member-states have much greater latitude in dealing with items listed under Category II. These include complete rockets and UAVs that are not covered in Category I – i.e., those capable of a range of 300km or more, whatever their payload. These complete systems were added under Category II in 1993 out of concern that biological weapons and chemical weapons – particularly the former – did not need a payload of anything like 500kg to achieve mass-destruction effects. This is especially true of cruise missiles and other UAVs, which are particularly adept at delivering such agents. The flood of non-weaponised UAVs coming onto the market requires close member scrutiny – not only as potential Category I systems, but as Category II items as well. (MTCR language on range/payload trade-offs applies equally to Category II systems, suggesting that payload reductions could enable many UAVs, and even ASCMs, to be modified to achieve at least a 300km range.)

Category II also includes a wide range of dual-use technologies, material and equipment items. Although much greater export latitude is permitted for Category II items, members must first determine that the items are not usable in a WMD-armed missile, nor in one that falls within Category I's 300km/500kg threshold.

Regime Implementation

The MTCR's export guidelines are implemented according to national legislation. Therefore, licensing and enforcement activities vary among member-states. The regime makes no provision for penalising member-states that violate its guidelines, but individual members can and do impose sanctions on violators unilaterally. Members meet at least once a year to discuss regime enhancements and to share intelligence on missile projects of concern. Numerous other inter-sessional consultations and technical experts' meetings occur throughout the year. All decisions are reached on a consensus basis.

Assessing the MTCR's Effectiveness

To consider the MTCR's effectiveness in controlling the spread of LACMs, at least three criteria should be assessed:[6]

- the degree of supplier participation;
- the consensus among members that cruise missiles are sufficiently dangerous to warrant cooperative controls; and
- member consensus on cruise-missile items that need to be controlled.

Supplier Participation

Full supplier participation is generally the most demanding criterion. But LACMs have not spread nearly as far as either ASCMs or ballistic missiles. The current MTCR membership includes most of the principal producers of cruise missiles and UAVs; there are, however, reasons to be concerned about the full participation of

Russia and China and their strict adherence to the MTCR's provisions.

Russia joined the MTCR as a full member in 1995 after a bitter controversy with the US over Russia's 1991 agreement to provide cryogenic rocket engines and related technology to India.[7] During the controversy Russia's MTCR status was that of an informal 'adherent' to the regime's guidelines – a category designed to encourage the observation of international norms on missiles and related technology transfers. But, even as Russia became a full member, controversy continued over reports not only of Russian exports for India's missile programme but of exports by Russian state entities for Iran's ballistic-missile programme.[8] Although Russia has striven to improve its system of national export controls, its announcement in mid-March 2001 of a new level of military-technical cooperation with Iran has fostered renewed concern about its future export behaviour.[9] Given the uncertainty over how the MTCR determines cruise-missile range, Russian marketing of several cruise missiles, including derivatives of the air-launched AS-15 (Kh-55) and the sea-launched 3M-55, deserves close scrutiny.

China's relationship with the MTCR is even more problematic. In becoming an 'adherent' to the MTCR's guidelines in October 1994, China took the unusual step of formulating its own version of precisely what adherence meant. China agreed to 'not export ground-to-ground missiles featuring the primary parameters of the MTCR'[10] – which suggests that its adherence applies only to complete Category I systems, not including air-to-ground cruise missiles. Moreover, this formulation does not acknowledge adherence to the MTCR's extensive annex of Category II items. In effect, China has explicitly rejected all revisions to the original 1987 version of the MTCR, most importantly those made in 1993 to deal with controls over delivery systems for biological and chemical agents (Category II, Item 19). Clearly, this formulation excludes many cruise missiles and other UAVs from any controls.

The deal announced on 21 November 2000 between China and the United States provides a useful illustration of China's problematic adherent status in the MTCR, particularly with respect to cruise-missile controls. In exchange for Washington's waiver of sanctions against Chinese 'entities' involved in missile-related exports to Pakistan and Iran, China undertook not to export nuclear-capable ballistic missiles and their technologies and to publish a specific export control list. (The United States also resumed normal consideration of applications to launch US satellites atop Chinese rockets.) Although the Clinton administration hailed the agreement as a major diplomatic milestone, nowhere in the text of either the Chinese or American statements was there a reference to cruise missiles. Instead, the State Department's official statement proclaimed: 'We welcome ... China's clear policy commitment not to assist, in any way, other countries to develop *ballistic* missiles that can be used to deliver nuclear weapons' (emphasis added).[11] Except for its promise to publish a control list of missile-related technologies, which is indeed a positive development, China's tendentious formulation of its adherence to the MTCR remains squarely in place.

Other potential suppliers of LACMs are not MTCR partner-states and are likely to remain so. If Russia and China prove unreliable MTCR partners and transfer complete systems and critical technologies (especially engines, stealth technologies and counter-measures) to, say, North Korea, Iran and Pakistan, the latter countries could establish a robust secondary market, just as they have done with ballistic missiles. A more advanced state such as India, with a proven cruise-missile capability, may simply decide to participate more aggressively in the export market than it has to date. New Delhi is already showing signs of targeting the Middle East market.[12] Still, the key to controlling the spread of the most advanced cruise missiles and related technologies lies in obtaining Russia's and China's adherence to the MTCR's full provisions.

Member Consensus on the Dangers of Cruise-missile Proliferation

The mere fact that the MTCR is a voluntary accord suggests that member-states desire to maintain some degree of flexibility in their export rights. While international norms against the acquisition of nuclear, biological and chemical weapons are reasonably robust, there is far less consensus on the need to control their means of delivery. Nonetheless, restraining the spread of missiles is a means of controlling WMD proliferation.

While international consensus against missile proliferation has yet to become firmly established, MTCR member consensus for restricting ballistic missiles is stronger than that for restricting cruise missiles or UAVs. However permissible their actions may have been, the export behaviour of key members demonstrates a greater willingness to export cruise missiles and other UAVs than ballistic missiles. Two examples illustrate the point. The US has transferred short-range ballistic missiles to just three developing countries, but has sold ASCMs to more than a dozen and reconnaissance drones world-wide.[13] France is reported to have sold ballistic missiles to just one developing nation, yet it has exported ASCMs to nearly 30 developing nations.[14]

Until recently, key member-states have repeatedly characterised the problem of missile proliferation as consisting almost exclusively of the spread of ballistic missiles. Cruise-missile proliferation received hardly a mention in any of the Clinton administration's numerous treatments of missile proliferation appearing in congressional testimony, major foreign policy speeches and policy proclamations on export controls.[15] Nor was the Bush (senior) administration's handling of UN Security Council Resolution 687 at the end of the 1991 Gulf War any more sensitive to what constitutes missile proliferation. The resolution demanded that Iraq destroy and never again produce, nuclear, chemical and biological weapons and their means of delivery. But the language dealing with delivery means referred only to ballistic missiles with a range greater than 150km. UAVs are mentioned in the monitoring plan only to the extent that they assist Iraq in acquiring ballistic missiles.[16] Although Iraq's subsequent transformation of manned trainer aircraft into UAVs capable of delivering a 200kg payload to more than 600km might have occurred regardless of Resolution 687's imprecise language, the incident underscores the importance of emphasising the danger of cruise-missile proliferation before, not after, it manifests itself in its most pernicious forms. During the first few months of the new administration of George W. Bush, there were indications that a more inclusive and even-handed treatment of the missile-proliferation threat was emerging, with explicit attention given to the dangers of cruise missiles.[17] But, given the consensus nature of MTCR deliberations, such inclusiveness and even-handedness must be reflected not only in the rhetoric but also in the export behaviour of the entire MTCR membership.

Member Consensus on Cruise-missile Controls

Reaching member consensus on the items to be controlled in any technology-denial regime is always difficult. The MTCR's authors found that delineating UAV-related items for control was a more challenging problem than identifying which ballistic-missile technologies to restrict.[18] Nonetheless, a consensus was reached, and is evident in the decision to make a 'presumption to deny' the export of certain cruise-missile systems and technologies. This language affects both complete systems and technologies 'intended' for use as, or in, a WMD-delivery system. But finding persuasive evidence of such intent is problematic at best. In light of the difficulty of discerning a recipient's end-use intentions, it seems clear that the MTCR's most restrictive 'presumption of denial' guidance will be more readily invoked to control exports of Category I items – that is, complete cruise missiles or UAVs capable of carrying 500kg payloads to range of at least 300km, as well as certain major subsystems for such missiles.

While a theoretical consensus may exist on the presumption to deny exports of cruise missiles exceeding the 500kg/300km threshold, putting this into practice has proved exceedingly difficult and potentially disruptive. In spite of the fact that the Anglo-French *Black Shaheen* cruise missile is capable of carrying a 500kg payload significantly more than 300km,[19] Paris and London have decided to sell the missile to the UAE. Both capitals argue that the *Black Shaheen* transfer presents no proliferation danger. As stipulated in the MTCR guidelines, on the rare occasion when a Category I item is exported, governments must obtain binding end-use assurances from the recipient that the missile will be used only as a conventional weapon and will not be re-exported to another state. But such assurances do little to alleviate the possible negative impact of the *Black Shaheen* transfer on the export behaviour of other key MTCR members and regime adherents, most notably Russia and China. To help shore up member consensus over precisely how the regime's provisions apply to cruise-missile transfers, technology experts from member-states met in Berlin on 4–6 July 2000 to discuss ways of reducing ambiguities over determining cruise-missile range as well as other possible limits on cruise-missile technologies.[20] So far, however, no new clarifications or improved language have been announced.

The Category I threshold is even more problematic in regard to potential transfers of unarmed UAVs. Precise data on the true one-way range and payload potential of UAVs are not readily available. Moreover, there is enormous room for trading-off range and payload weight against each other to alter UAV performance as weapons-carrying systems. Explosive growth in UAVs for surveillance and reconnaissance missions, as well as growing attention to the development of UCAVs, jeopardise any membership consensus about how to handle UAV transfers. This concern applies not only to Category I transfers, but even more to Category II systems capable of a range of 300km regardless of payload. It bears restating: nearly 80% of the unarmed UAVs examined in a recent study appear capable of exceeding the MTCR's 300km-range threshold.[21] Monitoring the transfer of such systems will require MTCR members to exert an extraordinary degree of vigilance and informed judgment over identifying which systems are subject to either Category I or II controls. And such informed judgment cannot occur in the absence of membership consensus on range/payload trade-offs with respect to cruise missiles and UAVs.

Providing an improved safety net to capture unwanted transfers of complete systems will not eliminate the flow of essential enabling technologies needed to build cruise missiles from scratch or to modify or upgrade UAVs and ASCMs. This is due to the MTCR's intentional exemption of critical Category II subsystems as long as they are intended to support manned-aircraft programmes. This creates a significant loophole for potential proliferating states: the structures, propulsion systems, autopilots and navigation systems used in manned aircraft are essentially interchangeable with those of cruise missiles and UAVs. Hence, cruise-missile development can be conducted under the auspices of a legitimate manned-aircraft programme. This makes it extremely difficult for intelligence agencies to gather critical information on the true state of the cruise-missile threat. Nevertheless, to the extent that membership consensus can be built around tightened controls restricting the proliferation of advanced systems and key subsystems, it would make threat calculation more predictable by forcing proliferating states to take longer paths to acquiring advanced cruise missiles.

Strengthening the Regime

An ounce of prevention is worth a pound of cure. But the MTCR has been anything but focused on the dangers of cruise-missile proliferation and the steps needed to prevent its spread, or at least delay its severity. Instead, for at least the last decade, expanded membership has preoccupied MTCR deliberations.[22] Growing from its original G-7 membership to 33 members has certainly increased the representational value of the MTCR and nominally broadened the notion of international norms against the spread of missiles capable of causing mass destruction. But the same decade has seen a revolution in the underlying technologies enabling the growth of cruise missiles for land attack, and this has created the conditions for transforming the missile-proliferation scene in the decade ahead. Unless the MTCR partners begin to focus more systematically on these conditions, the regime risks becoming an institutional anachronism, shorn of any appreciable capacity to cope with the spread of cruise missiles.

To have any positive effect on controlling the spread of cruise missiles, the MTCR membership should, without delay, strengthen the provisions of the regime in four specific ways by:

- creating a uniform set of ground rules for determining the range and payload of cruise missiles and UAVs;
- implementing tighter controls on stealthy cruise missiles;
- examining and implementing tighter controls on counter-measure technologies specially designed to enhance cruise-missile penetration; and
- broadening current MTCR parameters governing Category II controls on jet engines.

These recommendations deal directly with transfers of advanced missiles and related technologies that severely stress even the most sophisticated cruise-missile defences. In that respect, they greatly complement efforts to plan for and implement improved cruise-missile defences. They require urgent attention.

Two other matters also deserve attention. First, although there are no controls governing the acquisition of very light kit aircraft, the membership should examine whether it might be possible to bring commercially available UAV flight-control systems under some degree of case-by-case Category II review. If their acquisition remains unchecked, kit aircraft could become a serious proliferation problem.[23] Second, the membership should undertake a comprehensive assessment of the impact of unarmed UAVs and armed UCAVs on existing controls. Explosive growth in these systems is expected over the next two decades, and increased pressure to create more flexible rules governing their export is inevitable.[24]

Ground Rules for Determining Cruise-missile Range and Payload

If consistent national implementation of MTCR controls is to occur, there is no priority that MTCR members face that is more urgent than strengthening the ground rules for determining cruise missiles' range and payload. The existing rules on range, written primarily with ballistic missiles in mind, involve a straightforward calculation of such missiles' maximum range trajectory. Cruise-missile manufacturers frequently quote a missile's range using low flight profiles. But cruise missiles need not fly their entire mission using such profiles;[25] they can be launched at or reach a range-maximising altitude and then drop to a terrain-hugging profile when they become more susceptible to detection.[26] There are also several other factors that contribute to determining the true range and payload capability of cruise missiles and other UAVs.[27]

However complex these factors may appear, individually and in combination, they comprise a workable set of inputs for consistent implementation of MTCR controls on cruise missiles and UAVs.[28] The MTCR membership has examined the issue in the past, particularly in the aftermath of the Anglo-French decision to transfer the *Black Shaheen* cruise missile to the UAE. As yet, though, it has failed to reach consensus on such ground rules. Without them, the proliferation of advanced cruise missiles is inevitable.

Tighter Controls on Stealthy Cruise Missiles

Chapter 4 demonstrates that the application of stealth technology to cruise missiles gives them the same characteristics as the ballistic missiles that inspired the MTCR: difficulty of defence, short warning time and shock effect. Calls for tighter controls on stealthy cruise missiles are long-standing, but the membership has struggled to reach consensus on precisely what level of control to impose.[29] Because of their inherent risk, Category I systems are automatically subject to a strong presumption of denial. The best approach to controlling stealthy cruise missiles would be to subject those missiles with more than 300km range (which are presently covered by Category II controls) to the same presumption of denial as Category I missiles. Cruise missiles capable of such ranges need not carry 500kg payloads to represent an extremely dangerous proliferation threat. They are significantly more effective in delivering small biological and chemical payloads than even Category I ballistic missiles. Coverage should be tightened on such stealthy cruise missiles.

New Controls on Specially Designed Countermeasure Equipment

The addition of endgame countermeasure equipment, such as towed decoys or terrain-bounce jammers, can greatly complicate cruise-missile defences. Opportunities for such additions as these will rise as RCS values for cruise missiles fall lower and lower.[30] Since this equipment is also used to enhance manned-aircraft survivability, it would appear at first glance that any such items covered under Category II controls might legitimately be exported as part of a manned aircraft. But to achieve the intended synergy with stealthy cruise missiles, countermeasure devices must be specially designed or modified to harmonise them to their companion vehicle. This suggests that the membership should investigate precisely how the regime might be modified to bring such devices under control. The time to make such changes is now, before stealthy cruise missiles have become a prominent feature of missile proliferation.

Broadened Parameters Covering Jet Engines

The capability of a jet engine is the most critical variable in determining the range of a cruise missile. Commercial and military engines with slightly above 2,000lb of thrust are fully usable in cruise-missile development or conversion programmes, yet the MTCR currently does not subject them even to minimal control. Broadening the MTCR's current parameters covering jet engine thrust under Category II would impose only a slight administrative burden on export-control organisations to review licensing applications that are commonly used in manned-aircraft transfers. Such case-by-case review would greatly enhance the membership's capacity to monitor the diversion of jet engines to cruise missiles that have Category I capabilities.

Reinventing the MTCR: A Global Missile Treaty?

Formal and informal calls to turn the MTCR from a voluntary supplier's regime into a universal, legally binding treaty have persisted since the regime's creation in 1987. The most recent formal example was a Canadian proposal to MTCR members for a global ban on all ground-launched ballistic missiles with ranges of 300–5,500km; in an *ad hoc* meeting of MTCR members in 1995, this attracted little support and collapsed. Non-governmental experts have called for a zero-ballistic-missile treaty, banning all ballistic missiles everywhere. The most promising arms-control proposal is to widen the US–Soviet Intermediate-range Nuclear Forces (INF) treaty into a global pact.[31]

Proponents of such a treaty see the INF treaty's simplicity and clarity of purpose as especially appealing. They argue that, by taking an existing bilateral treaty banning all land-based ballistic and cruise missiles with ranges of 500–5,500km and transforming it into a global regime, the US and Russia could capture the moral high ground on missile proliferation. But whatever good might result from establishing a legal norm would be more than offset by several conspicuous shortcomings. Three stand out.

First, the INF treaty's lower range limit of 500km is too high to be helpful. It would fail to capture strategically significant cruise missiles with biological and chemical payloads, as well as many varieties of tactical ballistic missile.

Second, the treaty bans only ground-launched ballistic or cruise missiles tested or deployed for weapons delivery, and so would leave out, *inter alia*, air- and sea-launched missiles, unarmed UAVs and cruise missiles easily capable of exceeding the stipulation of 'standard design mode' range.

Third, upgrading the INF treaty's role would probably damage the MTCR's effectiveness. If the INF treaty were made into a global regime, it would become the premier missile non-proliferation instrument, thereby making the MTCR at best merely a supplementary tool for combating missile proliferation. Worse, precious years spent on turning the INF treaty into an effective global instrument would sap the intensity of the effort that is needed now to strengthen and forcefully implement the MTCR's existing provisions – particularly those pertaining to advanced cruise missiles. Because only a handful of major industrial states is capable of facilitating the proliferation of these missiles, it would be better if they invested their finite diplomatic capital in efforts that are more likely to bear fruit.

However useful legally binding norms against missile proliferation may be, it is difficult to conceive of one that could adequately address the problem of cruise-missile proliferation. The very features of cruise missiles and UAVs (small size, conversion potential, multiple uses, etc.) that make them difficult to manage under the MTCR virtually preclude satisfactory treaty negotiation, let alone verification. Enhancing the MTCR remains the best option for thwarting the proliferation of cruise missiles.

Conclusion

Prospects for Cruise-Missile Proliferation

Monitoring and countering the threat of cruise missiles during the first two decades of the twenty-first century will in some important ways be more challenging than was thwarting late-twentieth-century threats. Whereas Cold War defence planners faced a monolithic adversary whose behaviour and weapons-development activity was relatively predictable, a more complex threat environment confronts today's defence planners. The ultimate wild card is the ease with which developing countries might currently acquire sophisticated cruise missiles from major industrial nations, the MTCR notwithstanding.

Direct transfers of advanced cruise missiles, though, are more likely to be detected than the longer routes to acquiring cruise missiles. Less convenient methods of acquisition could therefore work to the advantage of an adversary. The propagation of commercially available dual-use technologies, combined with the globalisation of the aircraft industry, essentially means that any determined nation can quickly gain access to the underlying technologies needed to develop LACMs. The scope and sophistication of its indigenous skill base and the precise nature of foreign assistance will then drive the pace of its cruise-missile development. Foreign assistance is a particularly important factor, whether a nation chooses indigenously to develop cruise missiles from scratch, or to convert ASCMs, unarmed UAVs or small kit planes.

The indigenous development or technological conversion route may take longer than direct purchases, but it is still likely to provide less warning time to other countries than would the development of a ballistic-missile capability. With cruise missiles, unlike ballistic missiles, there is no need to test large rocket motors. Even more important, cruise missiles are easier to hide during their development, because proliferating states can readily intermingle them with legitimate aircraft and unarmed UAV purchases or production, making technical intelligence detection extremely difficult.

The predictability of the evolution of the cruise-missile threat is also complicated by a diverse set of cross-cutting incentives and constraints affecting proliferating states. Perhaps the strongest incentive is the decided advantage of LACMs over ballistic missiles, and even manned aircraft, for achieving military objectives. Indeed, their capacity for precise delivery makes them the weapon of choice not only for biological and chemical attacks, but also for conventional ones. Regional states facing any US-led coalition cannot expect to see their aircraft survive much beyond the first blow of any campaign. Yet cruise missiles, launched from a variety of survivable platforms, would enable such a state to mount a strategic air campaign with cruise (and ballistic) missiles without achieving air superiority. Here the military effectiveness of LACMs interacts closely with the growing vulnerability of Western-style force projection, especially its dependence on short-legged aircraft operating out of a few forward bases. The cost of even advanced cruise missiles is less than that of ballistic missiles, and large numbers of converted kit aircraft and UAVs could conceivably become affordable for proliferating states; this adds to their attraction.

Third-world motives for acquiring large inventories of ASCMs, beginning in the 1960s, could shed light on what may occur in the future with LACMs. Despite their significant expense (typically around $800,000), about 40 developing nations that lacked the prestige and operational utility of large military establishments came to see ASCMs as yielding a high payoff. One accurately placed ASCM could potentially achieve strategic results even against a major industrial power; Argentina's use of only a few French *Exocets* during the Falklands War against the British Royal Navy furnishes but one example.[1]

But these incentives must be tempered by an equally compelling set of disincentives. A regional adversary of the US could, without detection, use cruise missiles earmarked for regional war fighting to attack US territory from an offshore vessel, but in terms of deterrence the value of these weapons pales in comparison to possessing an intercontinental ballistic missile (ICBM). Another possible constraining factor is the philosophical and bureaucratic difficulty of fully integrating cruise missiles into third-world force structures dominated by aircraft, tanks and ships. But perhaps the most important reason why cruise missiles have yet to spread widely is the absence in the US inventory of effective layered defences, including counter-force capabilities, against ballistic missiles. Not until after 2007 will such defences begin to be effectively deployed.

Conventional wisdom would suggest that the cruise-missile threat will evolve over time, from relatively few highly observable missiles in the near-term (1–5 years), via higher numbers of lower-observable, terrain-hugging missiles in the mid-term (5–15 years), to larger numbers of stealthy missiles with endgame countermeasures in the long term (15+ years). But major features of the long-term threat could materialise much sooner if the MTCR's handling of cruise-missile transfers does not improve, or if US–Russian and US–Chinese relations worsen. In either case, it is conceivable that modest numbers of stealthy cruise missiles with countermeasures, accompanied by large numbers of cheap, slow-flying UAVs or converted kit planes, could emerge in 5–10 years. Progress in US cruise-missile defences seems unlikely to keep pace with even the slowly evolving threat, much less the accelerated version. Were US and allied theatre air and missile defences to be tested in combat, they would not be capable of repelling combined ballistic- and cruise-missile attacks within this time frame.

Dealing with the Threat

Dealing with the threat of cruise missiles will require a true transformation in defence planning and non-proliferation policy. Signs of a willingness to shake up the US armed forces and the weapons they use are already evident in the new US administration of George W. Bush. Before conducting its congressionally mandated

Quadrennial Defense Review, President Bush's new Secretary of Defense, Donald Rumsfeld, commissioned a fundamental review of the US military's strategy, structure and missions.[2] The strategy review, led by Andrew W. Marshall, puts a premium on the military's ability to fight in regions where it either lacks access to bases or must operate from difficult-to-defend bases with short-range aircraft. Proliferation concerns emphasised in the review include advanced cruise missiles, quiet diesel submarines and nuclear, chemical and biological weapons. These threats, the review argues, will make force projection more susceptible to attack.[3] This vulnerability clearly implies a need for more effective defences and for greater reliance on longer-range stand-off weapons, such as the B-2 bomber and cruise missiles fired from submarines.

But the path from broad strategy guidelines to a true transformation in defence policy is fraught with pitfalls, not least of which is fierce service opposition to changes in traditionally favoured programmes. It appears likely, however, that the Rumsfeld-led Pentagon will cut back or kill several of these pet programmes to find as much as $3bn annually for its intended overhaul of the military. Some technology-development programmes for improved cruise-missile defence also could benefit from reprogrammed allocations. But it is even more important for disciplined advocates in key military and civilian leadership positions to march the services through the inevitable battles over service roles and missions, and to guide the development of new doctrine and concepts of operation for counter-force and joint theatre air and missile defence.[4] Finally, any notion of a single integrated air picture must include coalition partners, but such inclusion requires a determined and persistent US willingness to engage partners in working through the difficult details.

Transforming leadership is no less important in non-proliferation policy. For too long, advocacy for and implementation of MTCR policy in US decision-making has been primarily a mid-level bureaucratic responsibility in both the Pentagon and the State Department. If non-proliferation policy is truly to complement reinvigorated defence planning for improved cruise-missile defences, it will require the attention of senior decision-makers, as well as more rigorous and sustained management of the inter-agency process by the National Security Council. Committed senior leadership is also essential to forge changes in MTCR policy, which requires consensus among 33 partner-states. Leaders of key MTCR states must come together to convince this broad partnership of the benefits of enhanced MTCR controls on cruise-missile proliferation. If regime partners can be convinced that the spread of these missiles to regions of common vital interest is undesirable, modest efforts to strengthen the MTCR will be feasible. In the absence of these changes, an uncertain proliferation setting could significantly increase strategic instability.

Appendix

Selected Cruise-Missile Systems and Programmes

System	Type	Range (km)• Payload (kg)	Status
China			
HY-4 *Silkworm*	ASCM/LACM	160+•500	In service?
Hong Niao-1	LACM	400–600•400+	In service
Hong Niao-2	LACM	1,500–2,000•400+	In service?
Hong Niao-3	LACM	2,500•400+	Dev
France			
Apache-A	LACM	140+•520	Dev
Storm Shadow	LACM	350+•400+	Dev (a)
SCALP-EG	LACM	400–600•400+	Dev
Germany			
Taurus KEPD-150	LACM	150–250•400+	Dev (b)
Taurus KEPD-350	LACM	200–350•400?	Dev (b)
India			
Lakshya	UAV/LACM?	600•450	Dev
Israel			
Popeye Turbo	LACM	300+•?	Dev
Iran			
C-802	ASCM/LACM?	160+•165	In service
Iraq			
L-29	UAV/LACM	600•200	In service

System	Type	Range (km)• Payload (kg)	Status
North Korea			
AG-1(HY-2mod)	ASCM/LACM?	160•500	In service
Russia			
Yakhont 3M-55	ASCM	300•200	Dev
Club 3M-54E1	ASCM/LACM	300•200	Dev
Kh-55 (AS-15)	LACM	3,000•450+	In service
Kh-65	LACM	500•410	Dev
Kh-65E	LACM	280•400+	Dev
South Africa			
MUPSOW	LACM	200+•?	Dev
Torgos	LACM	300•500	Dev
UAE			
Black Shaheen	LACM	300+•450?	Dev (a)
UK			
Storm Shadow	LACM	350+•400+	Dev (a)
Tomahawk	LACM	1,650•320	In service
US			
Tomahawk BGM-109	LACM	1,000–2,500•450	In service
Tactical *Tomahawk*	LACM	1,650•450	Dev
AGM-86C	LACM	2,000•450	In service
JASSM	LACM	370•450	Dev

Notes

ASCM anti-ship cruise missile **LACM** land-attack cruise missile **Dev** Development **(a)** Jointly developed by France and the UK **(b)** Jointly developed with Sweden and Italy

Sources National Air Intelligence Center, *Ballistic and Cruise Missile Threat*, NAIC-1031-0985-99 (Dayton, OH: Wright-Patterson Air Force Base, September 2000) and author interviews with missile analysts and former government and industry officials.

Notes

Acknowledgements

The author would like to thank Dr Gregory DeSantis for his helpful advice on various technical issues examined in this Paper, and Dr Thomas Mahnken, Scott McMahon, Dr Richard Speier and Jonathan Stevenson for their advice and comments. The author, however, bears full responsibility for the Paper.

Introduction

1 This Paper is primarily concerned with cruise missiles for land-attack missions. To the extent that it addresses anti-ship cruise missiles (ASCMs), this is in order to evaluate their conversion to land-attack roles. Cruise missiles, or unmanned aerial vehicles (UAVs) and kit aircraft adapted to carry weapons, are fitted with aerodynamic surfaces that provide lift to keep them aloft during their entire flight (unlike air-to-surface missiles such as the AGM-65 *Maverick*, which have small fins to provide stability, rather than lift). In contrast to cruise missiles, ballistic missiles shed their rocket motors once these have propelled them outside the atmosphere; thereafter they pursue an unpowered ballistic course to their point of impact.

2 Lawrence Freedman, *The Revolution in Strategic Affairs*, Adelphi Paper 318 (London: Oxford University Press for IISS, 1998), p. 70.

3 Lt-Col. Jeffrey McCausland, *The Gulf Conflict: A Military Analysis*, Adelphi Paper 282 (London: Brassey's for the IISS, 1993), p. 53.

4 The most coherent and detailed military analysis of the Gulf War from the perspective of the developing world is Brig. Gen. V. K. Nair, *War in the Gulf: Lessons for the Third World* (New Delhi: Lancer International, 1991). For Nair's appraisal of the value of imposing costly penalties, see pp. 225–6.

5 Dennis M. Gormley, 'Hedging Against the Cruise-Missile

Threat', *Survival*, vol. 40, no. 1 (spring 1998), pp. 95–6.

6 Britain's performance against the V-1 and Gen. Eisenhower's assessment are cited in Richard K. Betts, 'Innovation, Assessment, and Decision', in Richard K. Betts (ed.), *Cruise Missiles: Technology, Strategy, Politics* (Washington DC: Brookings Institution, 1981), p. 5.

7 The consequences of this threat are usefully analysed in John Stillion and John Orletsky, *Air Base Vulnerability to Conventional Cruise Missile and Ballistic Missile Attacks: Technology, Scenarios, and US Air Force Response* (Santa Monica, CA: RAND Corporation, 1999).

8 See Michael G. Vickers, *Warfare in 2020: A Primer* (Washington DC: Center for Strategic and Budgetary Assessments, 1996), p. 5.

9 National Air Intelligence Center, *Ballistic and Cruise Missile Threat* (Wright-Patterson Air Force Base, OH: September 2000), p. 23.

Chapter 1

1 Joseph Farah, 'Why Iraq Is Buying Up Sony PlayStation 2's', http://www.sightings.com/general6/whyiraq.htm, 9 December 2000.

2 US air strikes during *Operation Desert Fox* in December 1998 attempted to target these Iraqi UAVs. Michael Eisenstadt, 'Iraq's Weapons of Mass Destruction (WMD): An Emerging Challenge for the Bush Administration', *Policywatch*, no. 515, vol. 26 (January 2001).

3 Author interview with Dr Gregory DeSantis, independent consultant.

4 Betts, 'Innovation, Assessment, and Decision', p. 4.

5 The best popular description of GPS is Michael Specter, 'No Place To Hide', *New Yorker*, 27 November 2000, p. 96ff. For technical details, see *Federal Radio Navigation Plan, 1990*, PB-91-190868 (Washington DC: US Department of Commerce, 1990). For a fair assessment of some of its military implications, see Raffi Gregorian, 'Global Positioning Systems: A Military Revolution for the Third World?' *SAIS Review*, vol. 13, no. 4, winter/spring 1993, pp. 133–48.

6 Accuracy is defined differently for GPS and for missile delivery. Take the example of an accuracy of 100m. In the case of missiles, the figure is defined in terms of circular error probable (CEP): the probability that 50% of the missiles will land within a circle of 100m diameter centred on the target. In the case of GPS, by contrast, this accuracy figure means that at least 95% of the time the position information reported is within 100m of its true position. In other words, a 100m GPS accuracy equates to a 40m CEP for a missile.

7 The JDAM munition has achieved a CEP of 9.6m, according to its manufacturer, Boeing.

8 Its future prospects are uncertain, due to Russia's current economic turmoil and to the changing fortunes of the Russian military. See Ivan Safronov, 'Uragan Heads for Space', *Moscow Kommersant*, 14 October 2000, p. 3 (FBIS translated text).

9 Accurate stand-alone, INS for commercial aircraft cost roughly $150,000. Less accurate stand-alone INS cost a third of this, but

adding embedded GPS receivers makes them far more accurate than the more expensive stand-alone INS. For an insightful treatment of this issue, see Steve Wooley, 'Proliferation of Precision Navigation Technologies and Security Implications for the US', Presentation to the Proliferation Countermeasures Working Group, Washington DC, 9 December 1991 (Alexandria, VA: Institute for Defense Analyses, 1991).

10 For a useful assessment of the military implications of commercial satellite imagery, see John C. Baker and Dana J. Johnson, 'Security Implications of Commercial Satellite Imagery', in John C. Baker, Kevin M. O'Connell and Ray A. Williamson (eds), *Commercial Observation Satellites: At the Leading Edge of Global Transparency* (Santa Monica, CA: RAND and the American Society for Photogrammetry and Remote Sensing, 2001), pp. 101–33.

11 In effect, this approach is a form of terrain profile matching, in which readings from the altimeter are continuously compared with predicted data from the strip-map.

12 Air-breathing gas turbines, which propel cruise missiles at subsonic speeds, are assumed here to be better propulsion choices than either solid-fuelled rockets or ramjets. Solid-fuelled rockets are heavy and only produce relatively short ranges compared with air-breathing engines. Ramjets need supersonic airflow to operate; thus they too are not only heavy but also depend upon a rocket booster or an aircraft to propel them to the speed of sound (Mach 1) before the ramjet takes over. Obviously, ramjet-propelled cruise missiles are readily detectable due to the enormous heat they produce, and the trade-off between supersonic and subsonic systems is one between speed and stealth. For a useful layman's treatment of cruise-missile propulsion choices, see David Tanks, *Assessing the Cruise Missile Puzzle: How Great a Defense Challenge?* (Washington DC: Institute for Foreign Policy Analysis, 2000), Appendix A.

13 Duncan Lennox, 'China's New Cruise Missile Programme "Racing Ahead"', *Jane's Defence Weekly*, 12 January 2000, p. 12.

14 The MTCR's technology annex (Item 3, Propulsion Components and Equipment) restricts, among other things, highly fuel-efficient turbine engines capable of producing at least 225lb of thrust, but excludes civil-certified engines producing a maximum thrust of more than 2,000lb.

15 *Report of the Commission to Assess the Ballistic Missile Threat to the United States, Executive Summary* (Washington DC: USGPO, 1998), pp. 6–7.

16 Tom Clancy and Russell Seitz, 'Nuclear Ubiquity: The End of Atom Secrecy', *Washington Post*, 5 January 1992, p. 1(C).

17 Lu Te-yung, 'Mainland Military Expert Visiting US Discloses that Mainland has Invited Experts of Former Soviet Union to Develop Cruise Missiles', *Lien Ho Pao* (Hong Kong), 30 July 1995, p. 8 (FBIS Translated Text). This report generally seems consistent with a 1995 Russian document discussed in Lennox, 'China's New Cruise Missile Programme'.

18 The upgrade also encompasses the tank's main gun and a new

diesel engine, transmission, gearbox and final drive. 'Iran: Building an Armor Industry', *Jane's Defence Weekly*, 23 October 1996, p. 23.

19 Anthony H. Cordesman, *Iranian Arms Transfers: The Facts* (Washington DC: CSIS, 15 October 2000), pp. 7, 13.

20 India has had little success in merging elements of the indigenous private sector's robust industrial capabilities into the government-run defence establishment. See K. Subrahmanyam, 'Self-reliant Defence and Indian Industry', Sixth Kiroloskar Memorial Lecture, www.idsa-india.org/an-oct-oo-2.html.

21 Atul Aneja, 'Go in for Cruise Missiles', on-line edition of *The Hindu*, distributed by www.indiaserver.com, 20 April 2000.

22 Tanks, *Assessing the Cruise Missile Puzzle*, p. 13. So far, the Indian press has only spoken of the *Lakshya*'s prospects as a training vehicle, but its coverage hints strongly at additional 'applications'. See, for example, Anantha Krishnan, 'India's Pilotless Aircraft Likely to Be Star Attraction at Republic Day Parade', *The Times of India* (Bombay) in English 21 Jan 2001 (FBIS transcribed text). For technical details on the new Indian turbojet engine, see 'India-Made Remote Controlled Jet Engine Tested Successfully', *The Hindu* (Chennai), 24 January 2001 (FBIS translated text).

23 For more on South African programmes, see National Air Intelligence Center, *Ballistic and Cruise Missile Threat*, p. 24 and Tanks, *Assessing the Cruise Missile Puzzle*, p. 16.

24 Author interview with a government official in Washington DC, April 2001. See also Tanks, *Assessing the Cruise Missile Puzzle*, p. 15.

25 Duncan Lennox reports that China began an experimental programme as long ago as 1977. See Lennox, 'China's New Cruise Missile Programme'.

26 For details of Iranian cruise-missile development, see Cordesman, *Iranian Arms Transfers*, pp. 26–7.

27 K. Scott McMahon and Dennis M. Gormley, *Controlling the Spread of Land-Attack Cruise Missiles* (Marina del Rey, CA: American Institute for Strategic Cooperation, 1995), pp. 50–51.

28 Michael R. Gordon, 'North Korea Tests Cruise Missile Designed to Sink Ships', *New York Times*, 1 June 1994, p. A12, and Duncan Lennox, (ed.)., 'Unclassified Projects: Offensive Weapons', *Jane's Strategic Weapon Systems*, issue 19 (Coulsdon: Jane's Information Group, September 1995).

29 This is a key theme developed in Richard A. Bitzinger, *False Promises, Failed Dreams, and Lowered Expectations: The Second-Tier Arms-Producing Countries in the 21st Century* (forthcoming).

30 *Report of the Commission to Assess the Ballistic Missile Threat to the United States*, p. 7.

Chapter 2

1 Much of the original *Harpoon*, including the airframe, propulsion system and fire-control system (FCS), survived its transformation into SLAM. What did change was the addition of a GPS guidance

adjunct for mid-course updates, new terminal seekers (optical and IR) to replace the original radar seeker, and a larger payload (the *Tomahawk* warhead).

2 The US Navy subsequently upgraded SLAM with an extended-range variant that more than doubles the original SLAM's 120km range. This was achieved by extending the missile's sustainer section by 23.2in for additional fuel. For additional details, see McMahon and Gormley, *Controlling the Spread of Land-Attack Cruise Missiles*, pp. 55–6.

3 Lennox, 'Unclassified Projects: Offensive Weapons'.

4 Steven J. Zaloga, 'The Cruise Missile Threat: Exaggerated or Premature?' *Jane's Intelligence Review*, April 2000, pp. 47–51. Zaloga notes that about 65% of the cost typically goes to the guidance and flight controls, 10% to the warhead, 20% to propulsion, and only 5% to the airframe.

5 The Chinese *Silkworm*, rather than the Russian *Styx*, is selected for evaluation simply because it is more often found in developing nations' inventories.

6 Many nations possessing inventories of ASCMs are either upgrading or acquiring a new generation of missile to meet modern requirements. For more on this phenomenon, see Lon O. Nordeen, 'Antiship Missiles Create New Challenges', *Proceedings*, vol. 127, January 2001, pp. 87–9.

7 In a 1994 finding supporting the Department of Defense's opposition to a Commerce Department approval to sell US turbofan engines to China, the intelligence community argued that China could use the engines

to upgrade the *Silkworm* to carry a 450kg payload to a range of about 600km. Jack Anderson and Michael Binstein, 'Worrisome Engine Sales to China', *Washington Post*, 9 May 1994, p. 14(C). For a detailed account of the controversy surrounding the sale of Garrett turbofan engines to China, see *Report of the Select Committee on US National Security and Military/Commercial Concerns with The People's Republic of China*, House of Representatives Report 105-851, 105th Congress, 2d Session (Washington DC: USGPO, 1999).

8 Zaloga, 'The Cruise Missile Threat', pp. 47–51.

9 The author is grateful to Dr Gregory DeSantis for his able assistance in considering how one would approach the design and construction of a suitable land-attack navigation system for the *Silkworm* missile.

10 By lengthening the fuselage about a 1m for additional fuel cells, the missile could fly an additional 200km, and even more if some of the missile's heavy payload (500kg) were traded off to provide for even more fuel. Extending the airframe would be a moderately complex task, but one that countries like Iraq, North Korea and several others have routinely practised to extend the range of their ballistic missiles. Overall structural modifications to the *Silkworm* would include making bulkheads or partitions between compartments and riveting simply shaped aluminium plates to increase the missile's length.

11 Flight-path programming is complicated. To enhance the prospect of penetrating air defences, the most effective

approach for low-level flight would be to make use of the earth's curvature and of the terrain along the chosen flight path so as to minimise radar detection. Rather than programming the missile to fly at a commanded altitude from way point to way point, the missile would be programmed to fly different glide slopes between each way point in accordance with digital terrain elevation information derived from satellite imagery and radar altimeter inputs. Generally speaking, if the terrain to the target is marked by great variation in altitude, then the burden of mission planning is correspondingly increased (because more way points and calculated glide slopes are needed). Conversely, relatively unvaried terrain would mean that the missile could be simply programmed to fly a commanded altitude.

[12] It is important to note that this time-line assumes that a country interested in achieving a reliable system capable of significant delivery accuracy will employ a rough approximation of the Western systems-engineering process. This differs from the basic premise of the 1998 Rumsfeld Commission that a developing country could compress development time for a long-range ballistic missile by reducing or eliminating the need for stiff systems-engineering standards of high system reliability and performance.

[13] 'Prospects for Unmanned Aerial Vehicles', *IISS Strategic Comments*, vol. 6, issue 7, September 2000.

[14] David Mulholland, 'Study: World UAV Market to Boom in Coming

Years', *Defense News*, 29 June–5 July 1998, p. 1.

[15] Gormley, 'Hedging Against the Cruise-Missile Threat', p. 97, and McMahon and Gormley, *Controlling the Spread of Land-Attack Cruise Missiles*, pp. 45–66.

[16] Yitshak Shichor, 'Israel's Transfers to China and Taiwan', *Survival*, vol. 40, no. 1, spring 1998, p. 90.

[17] Gregory DeSantis and Steven J. McKay, *Unmanned Aerial Vehicles: Technical and Operational Aspects of an Emerging Threat*, PSR Report 2839 (Arlington, VA: Veridian-Pacific-Sierra Research, 2000). This study was sponsored by the US Defense Advanced Research Projects Agency and prepared under contract to the Electronic Systems Center, US Air Force Material Command, Hanscom Air Force Base, MA.

[18] More specifically, the model includes two parts: an analytical solution to the thrust $v.$ drag equation to obtain flight performance curves; and a set of empirical equations based on a large sample set of UAVs for other physical characteristics, such as wing area, fuel/payload ratio, fuel consumption and engine power (thrust or horsepower). *Ibid.*, p. 18.

[19] Nearly 65% were powered by reciprocating rather then gas-turbine engines. Indeed, perhaps for reasons of cost, four times more propeller-driven UAVs than gas-turbine models are being acquired. *Ibid.*, p. 12. This study notes that propeller-driven UAVs are roughly one-tenth the cost of rocket-powered or gas-turbine UAVs.

[20] Many little explosions on a large soft target are much more effective than one large

detonation of equivalent high explosive – by about a factor of 3 for a 30kg payload and a factor of nearly 8 for a 450kg payload. See Stillion and Orletsky, *Air Base Vulnerability*, pp. 11–12.

21 For a list of manufacturers and links to their web sites, see www.sportflyer.com/ kitplane.htm.

22 The current unit cost of one Patriot PAC-3 missile is $5m. See Robert Holzer and Gopal Ratnam, 'Missile Defense on Budget Battlefield', *Defense News*, 22 January 2001, p. 1.

23 Just such a scenario is painted in Stillion and Orletsky, *Air Base Vulnerability*, p. 17.

24 Information on Russian marketing activities is derived from author interviews with attenders at the 1992 Moscow Air Show and the 1993 IDEX Defence Exhibition in Abu Dhabi.

25 Tanks, *Assessing the Cruise Missile Puzzle*, p. 11.

26 The most explicit and thorough reporting on Chinese cruise-missile developments comes from Duncan Lennox of Jane's Information Group and Maj. Mark A. Stokes, former assistant US air attaché in China. See Lennox, 'China's New Cruise Missile Programme "Racing Ahead"', and Mark A. Stokes, *China's Strategic Modernization: Implications for the United States* (Carlisle, PA: US Army Strategic Studies Institute, September 1999), pp. 79–86.

27 Reflecting the recent consolidation and strategic partnering occurring in Europe, MBD is actually a joint-venture company owned by the European Aeronautic, Defence and Space Company (EADS) and Britain's BAe Systems. EADS includes Construcciones Aeronauticas, DaimlerChrysler Aerospace and Aérospatiale Matra.

28 'French Apache MSOW Takes Another Step Forward', *International Defense Review*, vol. 22, no. 10, October 1989, p. 1295.

29 For details of the *Apache* and its derivatives, see J. A. C. Lewis and Craig Hoyle, 'MBD hails Storm Shadow test success', *Jane's Defence Weekly*, 24 January 2001, p. 3 and Jean Dupont, 'Scalp Has Made Its First Firing', *Paris Air & Cosmos*, 19 January 2001, pp. 40–41 (FBIS translated text).

30 Author interviews with French MOD officials in June 1994. The longest-range variant of the *Apache* has been known variously as the *Super Apache*, the *Apache-C* and the *Apache APTGD* – i.e., *arme de précision tirée a grande distance* (long-range, high accuracy weapon). MBD is reported to have launched preliminary studies of new versions of the *Apache* family of missiles for naval and land missions. See 'Scalp in Land and Submarine Versions', *Air & Cosmos*, 24 December 2000, p. 44 (FBIS translated text).

31 Membership of MTCR does not entitle a country to purchase missiles from other member-states, and the behaviour of the MTCR member-states reflects a diversity of practices on intra-membership transfers. The Greek sale was somewhat controversial because of a concern in Washington about maintaining the military balance between Turkey and Greece.

32 Flight modelling demonstrates that even the shortest-range variant of the *Apache* will fly beyond 300km with a 500kg

payload by taking advantage of a higher flight altitude for a portion of its overall flight before going low for terminal survivability.

[33] Karl Schwarz, 'Stand-off Missiles Compared', *Stuttgart Flug Revue* (Internet version) in English, 1 April 2001 (FBIS translated text).

[34] Turkish officials responded to the announcement of the Greek purchase of *Storm Shadow* by stating that it strengthened their hand in seeking the purchase of the Israeli *Popeye* LACM. See Douglas Barrie and Christina MacKenzie, 'Matra BAe Court Greece to Buy New Cruise Missile', *Defense News*, 24 July 2000, p. 3.

[35] See, for example, Reuven Pedatzur, 'Facing the Sea', *Ha'aretz* (Tel Aviv), 12 January 2001, p. B1 (FBIS translated text).

Chapter Three

[1] See, for example, Janne E. Nolan, *Trappings of Power: Ballistic Missiles in the Third World* (Washington DC: Brookings Institution, 1991), pp. 14–20. For a more contemporary treatment of motivations to acquire ballistic missiles, see Ben Sheppard, 'Ballistic Missile Proliferation and the Geopolitics of Terror', *Jane's Intelligence Review*, December 1998, pp. 40–44.

[2] According to the authoritative *Gulf War Air Power Survey*, the Defense Intelligence Agency could not positively confirm the destruction of even one Iraqi ballistic missile launcher by US air attacks. That said, the round-the-clock air campaign against Iraqi missile launchers had the virtual effect of reducing the overall rate of fire of Iraqi *Scuds*. See *Gulf War Air Power Survey, Vol. II: Operations and Effects and Effectiveness* (Washington DC: USGPO, 1993), pp. 330–40.

[3] For an insightful account of the lessons learned and after-effects of Iraq's use of ballistic missiles, see K. Scott McMahon, *Pursuit of the Shield: The US Quest for Limited Ballistic Missile Defense* (Lanham, MD: University Press of America, 1997), pp. 77–79.

[4] For example, Brazilian military authorities drew attention not only to ballistic missiles, but also to precision weapons as two examples of weapon systems that could thwart a major power's intervention or provide decisive advantage over regional adversaries. See Domicio Proenca, Jr., 'Brazilian Perceptions of the Persian Gulf War of 1991: An Impressionistic View', study prepared for the Center for National Security Studies, Los Alamos National Laboratory conference on 'Gulf War Lessons Learned by Foreign Nations', Los Alamos, New Mexico, November 1991.

[5] McCausland, *The Gulf Conflict: A Military Analysis*, pp. 34, 36. Of course, one can only assume that fear of US retaliation affected Iraq's decision not to employ its WMD warheads. However, effectively delivering chemical and biological payloads on crudely designed ballistic missiles is highly problematic, and this may account for Iraqi behaviour.

[6] This calculation assumes that the cruise missile is flying at 800km per hour. See Gerald Frost and Irving Lachow, *Satellite Navigation-Aiding for Ballistic and Cruise Missiles*, RAND/RP-543

(Santa Monica, CA: RAND
Corporation, 1996), p. 11.

7   Generally, the lethality of such a
precision attack would depend
far more on knowing exactly
where the target is than on small
changes in CEP. High-resolution
commercial space imagery, or
differential GPS readings at or
near fixed targets, increases the
prospect that cruise missiles can
deliver highly lethal
conventional payloads. Apart
from knowing the target's precise
location, several other factors
contribute to the ultimate
lethality of any given attack,
including the cruise missile's
accuracy, the angle of its terminal
dive, its payload characteristics
and the size and hardness of the
target. *Ibid.*, pp. 12–13.

8   Frost and Lachow report a CEP
of 500–1,000m for the *Scud*-B and
1.5–3km for the North Korean
No-Dong 1. *Ibid.*, p. 4. For an
insightful treatment of missile
accuracy, see Gregory S. Jones,
*The Iraqi Ballistic Missile Program:
The Gulf War and the Future of the
Missile Threat* (Marina del Rey,
CA: American Institute for
Strategic Cooperation, summer
1992).

9   *Ibid.*, pp. 3–8.

10 For an advanced ballistic missile
like the Chinese M-9, this means
that one might expect GPS-aiding
to improve its original 600m CEP
down to around 150–200m.

11 Of course, larger ballistic missiles
will generally carry
correspondingly larger payloads
than cruise missiles.

12 See, for example, Nair, *War in the
Gulf*, pp. 139–40, and
McCausland, *The Gulf Conflict*,
p. 53.

13 David J. Nicholls, *Cruise Missiles
and Modern War: Strategic and*

Technical Implications, Occasional
Paper No. 13 (Maxwell AFB, AL:
Center for Strategy and
Technology, Air War College,
May 2000), p. 23.

14 While critical NATO air-defence
and nuclear-capable aircraft were
distributed among 20 air bases in
the Central Region during the
Cold War, during the Gulf War
literally thousands of aircraft
were jammed into (and parked
openly at) fewer than 10 air
bases, and during the Kosovo
campaign aircraft were primarily
concentrated at two bases. For
more on air-base vulnerability
during the Cold War, see Dennis
M. Gormley, *Double Zero and
Soviet Military Strategy:
Implications for Western Security*
(London: Jane's Publishing,
1988), chapters 3–5. On air-base
vulnerability in Saudi Arabia, see
Stillion and Orletsky, *Air Base
Vulnerability*, pp. 5–7. On Kosovo,
see Andrew Brookes, *Hard
European Lesson from the Kosovo
Air Campaign*, IFS Info 2/2000
(Oslo: Norwegian Institute for
Defence Studies, 2000), p. 8.
Brookes sensibly calls for a long-
term strategy for maintaining
contingency airfields.

15 For details of the RAND
Corporation scenario, see Stillion
and Orletsky, *Air Base
Vulnerability*, especially chapter 3.
The Chinese attack on Taiwan,
the author's own scenario,
appeared in abbreviated form in
Dennis Gormley, 'Defusing
China's Threat to Taiwan',
Defense News, 24 April 2000, p. 29.

16 These calculations assume a
lethal radius of 20ft for the 1lb
submunition and that 75% of the
payload weight is made up of
submunitions, the rest
representing frame and

dispensing mechanism. *Ibid.*, p. xiii.

17 The Chinese M-9 ballistic missile has a range of 600km and a payload of 500kg. The M-18 is essentially an M-9 with an extra booster state producing a range of around 900km with the same payload. RAND considered two UAV airframes for conversion: the US Lear R4E *Skyeye* (with a one-way range of over 1,100km and a payload of 80kg) and the Yugoslav SDPR VBL-2000 (with a range of just under 1,100km and a payload of 30kg), both of which are included in the large database of UAVs examined in DeSantis and McKay, *Unmanned Aerial Vehicles*.

18 That said, the RAND analysis shows the synergistic effect of combining cruise- and ballistic-missile attacks: the lightly armed cruise missiles attacked the missile defence's guidance radar stations, thereby leveraging the effectiveness of subsequent ballistic-missile attacks. Missile-defence batteries have little capability to engage such slow-flying cruise missiles. Stillion and Orletsky, *Air Base Vulnerability*, p. 25.

19 The RAND analysis estimated a cost of $200,000 and $300,000 for the two modified UAVs consider-ed in their scenario, though they acknowledge that they had limited information on the true cost of such modifications. As noted in Chapter 2, assuming a production run of several hundred units, modified kit planes can probably be produced for around $50,000 per missile.

20 Finally, while a Middle East scenario need not be concerned with problems of wing icing and vulnerability to ground fire for slow-flying UAVs, other scenarios might have to consider the use of a larger number of such slow fliers to insure that a given number penetrate to their targets.

21 Lt-Gen. Charles A. Horner, 'Combat Debriefing', *Cable News Network*, 21 January 1991. To be fair, predicting how the public would respond to such attacks is problematic at best.

22 The most effective way to disseminate chemical and biological agents lies in exploiting the cruise missile's aerodynamic flight stability. This permits the cruise missile to become a line-source means of delivery, releasing and spraying the agent at right angles to the wind direction and upwind of the target area, greatly increasing dissemination efficiency. See Edward Eitzen, 'Chapter 20 – Use of Bio Weapons', *in Medical Aspects of Chemical and Biological Warfare* (Washington DC: Walter Reed Army Medical Center, 1997), pp. 440–42. Ballistic missiles, by contrast, have much lower dissemination efficiencies. Due to their fast speeds and relative instability, they are point sources of dissemination; the agent is released by explosive or gaseous means and is disseminated at the point of impact, which increases the chance that some of the agent may be compromised during dissemination and that, compared with a line-source system, less agent overall ends up suspended in the atmosphere.

23 The release and subsequent effectiveness of chemical, and especially biological, agents are governed by a host of factors, including whether the agent is

dry or liquid, the height of release, speed of release, existing meteorological conditions (sunlight, wind speed, temperature, humidity) and the particular parameters of the target. Thus, predicting outcomes for chemical or biological attacks is far more difficult than for conventional or nuclear-weapon attacks.

[24] These calculations are taken from Gregory F. Treverton and Bruce W. Bennett, *Integrating Counterproliferation into Defense Planning*, RAND CF-132 (Santa Monica, CA: RAND Corporation, 1997), appearing at www.rand.org/publications/CF/CF132.

[25] William S. Cohen, *The Security Situation in the Taiwan Strait: Report to Congress Pursuant to the FY99 Appropriations Bill* (Washington DC: Department of Defense, 1999).

[26] *Ibid.*, p. 19.

[27] All Taiwan's *Mirage* 2000 air-defence aircraft (roughly 60) are housed at Hsinchu air base, while two other bases (Chiayi and Hualien) support around 120 F-16 air-defence/attack aircraft. See *Jane's All the World Air Forces*, issue 9 (Coulsdon: Jane's Publishing, August 1999).

[28] The runway cratering submunition is similar in design to the French KRISS submunition found on the *Apache* cruise missile. It consists of 10 51kg packages of submunitions each designed to penetrate concrete and temporarily prevent the repair of the damaged runway.

[29] See Gormley, *Double Zero and Soviet Military Strategy*, pp. 103–105, for background on and calculations of missile attacks on runways.

[30] Department of the Army, Office of the Deputy Chief of Staff for Operations and Plans, Force Development, Concepts, Doctrine, and Policy Division, 'Army Theater Missile Defense', briefing charts, US Department of the Army, mimeo, n.d.

[31] That said, the history of cruise-missile development programmes has included examples of huge overruns, most notably on the US Tri-Service Stand-off Attack Missile (TSSAM), which was cancelled in 1994 after expected unit costs tripled to some $2.4m.

[32] Cost data for each of the cruise missiles except *Silkworm* are taken from Nicholls, *Cruise Missiles and Modern War*. On *Silkworm*'s cost, see 'Chinese Anti-Ship Missiles', in *World Missiles Briefing* (Fairfax, VA: Teal Group Corporation, May 1995), p. 5.

[33] On *Scud* costs, see McMahon, *Pursuit of the Shield*, p. 74. For an estimate of the M-9's cost, see Stillion and Orletsky, *Air Base Vulnerability*, Appendix A, p. 79.

[34] See Nicholls, *Cruise Missiles and Modern War*. Nicholls compares $300,000 cruise missiles with $30m manned aircraft. Each aircraft carries four $20,000 JDAM weapons, the cost of aircraft operations and support is assumed to be twice the aircraft's procurement cost, and the aircraft is shot down halfway through its operational life cycle. Cruise-missile operations and support is 10% of the weapon's cost.

[35] Support for precise and discriminate technologies came to a head in the early 1970s in the Long Range R&D Study sponsored by the Pentagon's

Advanced Research Projects Agency. Of course, the advent of cheap guidance and control systems, manifested in GPS/INS technology, has greatly reduced the costs of such precision weapons.

[36] Iran continues to purchase foreign aircraft, trainers and air-to-surface missiles. Cordesman, *Iranian Arms Transfers*, p. 14.

[37] In late 2000 China launched two navigational satellites, indicating its intention to build its own GPS system. See Richard D. Fisher, 'Unsafe Without Aegis', *Wall Street Journal*, 25 April 2001, p. 20.

[38] Without anti-jam enhancements, a GPS-guided missile can be jammed (which breaks the satellite signal) at a range of 4.5km by a 1-watt noise ground-based jammer. Gerald Frost, *Operational Issues for GPS-Aided Precision Guided Weapons* (Santa Monica, CA: RAND Corporation, 1994), chapter 5.

[39] The best recent treatment of nuclear deterrence is Sir Michael Quinlan, *Thinking About Nuclear Weapons* (London: RUSI Whitehall Paper Series, 1997). On the erosion issue, see Dennis M. Gormley and Thomas G. Mahnken, 'Facing Nuclear and Conventional Reality', *Orbis*, winter 2000, pp. 109–25.

[40] See *Report of the Defense Science Board Task Force on Nuclear Deterrence* (Washington DC: Office of the Under Secretary of Defense for Acquisition and Technology, October 1998).

Chapter 4

[1] In the late 1950s and early 1960s, driven by the threat of Soviet intercontinental bombers, the US deployed thousands of manned interceptors, about 100 SAM batteries and hundreds of ground radar sites. The advent of the intercontinental ballistic-missile threat in the mid-1960s, and the enormous difficulty and cost of defending against them eliminated the rationale for significant strategic air defences. See William P. Delaney, 'Air Defense of the United States: Strategic Missions and Modern Technology', *International Security*, vol. 15, no. 1, summer 1990, pp. 181–211.

[2] John C. Toomay, 'Technical Characteristics', in Betts, *Cruise Missiles*, p. 32. Radar cross-section is an expression of the extent to which targets reflect radar pulses. The radar cross-section of a cruise missile can vary greatly, depending on the aspect of the cruise missile in relation to the radar transmitter. Radar reflection off the nose of the cruise missile, from a transmitter in the head-on position, usually yields the smallest radar cross-section, while a broadside presentation to the signal gives the greatest. Shape, surface roughness and reflective material as well as orientation also affect the radar cross-section. See M. Weik, *Communications Standard Dictionary*, 2nd ed. (New York: Van Nostrand Reinhold, 1989). RCS values included in the text assume nose-on orientations.

[3] Based on interviews with former government officials in Washington DC in December 2000 and January 2001. Air-fratricide problems caused by the need to defend against cruise missiles are likely to be most severe in the early stages of any

conflict – when only minimal surveillance and BMC3 systems are likely to be in place, and coordination among service air fleets and coalition partners is unlikely to have gelled.

4   AWACS performance is derived from Irving Lachow, *GPS-Guided Cruise Missiles and Weapons of Mass Destruction*, RP-463 (Santa Monica, CA: RAND Corp., 1995), pp. 11–13.

5   For a useful layman's view of radar performance against small targets, see Tanks, *Assessing the Cruise Missile Puzzle*, pp. 17–22.

6   The Medium Extended Air Defense System (MEADS) is advertised as not only adept at defending against ballistic missiles but cruise missiles as well. However, without linking it to a wide-area airborne sensor capable of furnishing fire-control quality information, MEADS' radar will suffer from the same horizon limitations as other sea- and ground-based SAM systems.

7   The late 1990s study, by the US Department of Defense's Advanced Research Projects Agency, is briefly referred to in DeSantis and McKay, *Unmanned Aerial Vehicles*, p. 9. The calculation of $4m per kill includes the costs of the missiles fired and assets (like launchers) used; one must imagine that a lower unit cost per *Patriot* missile was assumed (current costs have subsequently risen to some $5m per missile – see Holzer and Ratnam, 'Missile Defense on Budget Battlefield', p. 1).

8   David A. Fulghum, 'DARPA Tackles Kosovo Problems', *Aviation Week & Space Technology*, 2 August 1999, p. 55.

9   See Dennis M. Gormley, 'Counterforce Operations',

presentation at Royal United Services Institute for Defence Studies conference on 'Extended Air Defence and the Long-range Missile Threat', London, 17–18 September 1997.

10   On the state of counter-force, see 'USAF Theater Missile Defense Attack Operations, Briefing to Mr Dennis Gormley', HQ USAF/XORT, 21 January 1999, mimeo. See also Dennis M. Gormley and K. Scott McMahon, 'Who's Guarding the Back Door? The Neglected Pillar of US Theater Missile Defense', *International Defense Review*, vol. 29, May 1996, pp. 21–24.

11   This would include equipment for chemical decontamination and rapid runway repair.

12   Stillion and Orletsky, in *Air Base Vulnerability*, p. 31. Note that a single fighter-size aircraft shelter costs roughly $4m, so hardened shelters for five fighter wings would cost over $1.4bn.

13   For details see Bryan Bender, 'Defense Science Board Report Brands Cruise Missiles Increasing Threat', *Inside the Army*, vol. 7, 30 January 1995, p. 1; and Richard Lardner, 'Cruise Missile Defense Group Recommends AWACS, E-2C Upgrades', *Inside Missile Defense*, vol. 1, no. 4, 8 November 1995, pp. 1, 6–7.

14   Section 274 of the *National Defense Authorization Act for Fiscal Year 1996* (Washington DC: USGPO, 1995), pp. 59–60.

15   Dennis Gormley, 'Cruise Missile Threat Rises: US Navy, Army Lag in Defense Preparations', *Defense News*, 31 May 1999, p. 15.

16   These observations on the state of cruise-missile defence are based in part on interviews conducted between December

2000 and February 2001 with current and former US Department of Defense and industry officials.

[17] Daniel G. Dupont, 'Joint Theater Air and Missile Defense Organization May Be Terminated', *Inside Missile Defense*, vol. 6, no. 17, 23 August 2000, pp. 3–4.

[18] These investments would position the services to enter engineering and manufacturing development: that phase of development that deals with fixing the design, determining cost, reducing risk and possibly full-rate production.

[19] According to the US Government Accounting Office (USGAO), correctly defining the threat is mentioned repeatedly in its interviews with government officials as a major challenge to prioritising cruise-missile defence spending. See *Cruise Missile Defense: Progress Made But Significant Challenges Remain*, GAO/NSIAD-99-68 (Washington DC: USGAO, March 1999), p. 17.

[20] The Defense Science Board's seminal 1994 study posited a threat evolution consisting of 'now', with essentially no threat from LACMs; 'soon' (roughly the equivalent of the mid-term threat, but commencing shortly after 1995) and 'later', with very-low-cross-section missiles and endgame countermeasures emerging before 2010. Interview with industry official, January 2001. Clearly, the threat has not emerged with increasing levels of severity. However, the irony is that the 'later' part of this prediction may still prove accurate if advanced Russian and Chinese cruise missiles are not subjected to MTCR controls.

[21] According to Dr Theodore Gold, Chairman of the first of two Defense Science Board studies on cruise-missile defence, various defence acquisition regulations warrant the expenditure of resources when the threat is anticipated rather than formally validated. Interview with Dr Gold on 22 December 2000.

[22] The 1996 and 1997 departures from the Pentagon of, respectively, Admiral William Owens, former Vice Chairman of the Joint Chiefs of Staff, and Paul Kaminski, former Under Secretary for Acquisition and Technology, had a palpable adverse effect on leadership where cruise-missile defence is concerned.

[23] Various service or joint data-link programmes exist. For example, the US Air Force-led Joint Tactical Information Distribution System (JTIDS) is a communications, navigation and identification system intended to support theatre surveillance, identification, air control, weapons engagement coordination and direction. The US Navy Cooperative Engagement Capability (CEC) permits ship-borne, airborne and land-based radars to create a fully integrated track-quality view of air threats.

[24] The GAO points out that SIAP has suffered from limited budgets. See *Cruise Missile Defense*, p. 15.

[25] Chris Strohm, 'Lack of Integrated Air Picture May Create Problems for Developers', *Inside Missile Defense*, vol. 6, no. 26, 27 December 2000, pp. 10–11.

[26] Catherine MacRae, 'Working Toward Single Integrated Air Picture Capability', *Inside the*

Pentagon, 14 December 2000, pp. 1, 12–13.

[27] The principal alternative options to using airborne sensors have either performance or operational weaknesses. Space-based radar faces extraordinary technical challenges against low-RCS cruise missiles, as do over-the-horizon radars. Large numbers of surface-based and netted sensors have deployment and maintainability limitations.

[28] For details see Matthew Ganz, Defense Research Projects Agency, 'Cruise Missile Defense', briefing presented at Royal United Services Institute for Defence Studies conference on 'Extended Air Defence and the Long-range Missile Threat', London, 17–18 September 1997.

[29] It should be noted that such mission support requires dedicating the platform to such a task.

[30] The US Navy's E-2C *Hawkeye* airborne surveillance platform, based on carriers, is probably too small for such a role. (However, the E-2C requires upgrading to cope with detecting low-RCS cruise missiles, particularly if the Navy is to participate significantly in littoral or land warfare.) To enhance its surveillance mission against very-low-RCS cruise missiles, the US Air Force may have to consider upgrading AWACS beyond its current radar system improvement programme.

[31] 'New Radar Would Meld AWACS, J-STARS Roles', *Aviation Week & Space Technology*, 12 June 2000, pp. 29–30.

[32] The JLENS programme envisages using two aerostats, one performing surveillance out to 250km range, the other providing precision tracking to 150km range. For a useful account of JLENS, see Tanks, *Assessing the Cruise Missile Puzzle*, pp. 26–8.

[33] Even JSTARS would have some terrain masking limits in areas with mountainous terrain like Korea, although its radar acuity would most likely be greater than that being developed for JLENS.

[34] The relative cost estimate is taken from Tanks, *Assessing the Cruise Missile Puzzle*, p. 28.

[35] These impressions were gained from interviews in December 2000 and January 2001.

[36] Stillion and Orletsky, *Air Base Vulnerability*, pp. 30–42 treat this subject in detail.

[37] *Ibid.*, pp. 45–7.

[38] *Ibid.*, p. 45.

[39] Besides air-defence missiles, the US Navy's *Phalanx* anti-missile gun system could be modified to engage such targets. The advantage of a missile over a gun, though, is that the missile can engage such targets at longer ranges.

[40] Eliminating the seeker's costly gimbal assembly would greatly reduce the overall cost. For details on the technical approaches now being investigated under the DARPA Low Cost Cruise Missile Defense (LCCMD) Programme, see www.darpa.mil/spo/programs/lowcostcruisemissiledefense.htm.

[41] The LCCMD programme is investigating using a derivative of the Miniature Air Launched Decoy (MALD) as the interceptor vehicle. The MALD objective is to produce a cheap air vehicle with an average cost of $30,000 per vehicle, assuming a buy of 3,000 units.

[42] Focusing on the missile launcher

here ought not to suggest that attacks against supporting infrastructure are any less important. The US Air Force approach to targeting views cruise and ballistic missiles and their launchers as one among many time-critical ground targets against which reconnaissance and attack resources must be allocated. The approach is a decidedly *ad hoc*. See Gormley and McMahon, 'Who's Guarding the Back Door?' p. 22.

[43] The Pentagon-sponsored Joint Advanced Warfighting Program at the Institute for Defense Analyses has reached roughly the same conclusion. Its studies indicate that any improvement in counter-force targeting will depend heavily on creating and maintaining a specially organised, standing joint capability dedicated to mobile-missile targeting. See Col. Jack A. Jackson, 'USJFCOM's First Joint Experiment: Attack of Critical Mobile Targets', presentation to a SMi Ltd conference on 'Network Centric Warfare', 4–5 October 2000, London.

[44] Jointly sponsored by DARPA, the US Air Force and the National Reconnaissance Office, *Discoverer II* lost its congressional backing in late 2000 and no longer exists as a formal programme. The objective of the programme was to demonstrate the feasibility, utility and cost effectiveness of space-based ground moving target indicator capabilities via a series of experiments and demonstrations. These were to serve as a proof of concept for a large constellation of such satellites. Service interest remains strong, and the expectation is that the programme might be resurrected in the near future.

[45] Such marginal improvements would largely pertain to exploiting ballistic missiles' launch signatures and backtracking to launch locations. This could not be applied to cruise missiles, due to their small launch signature.

[46] In fact, a US bipartisan panel assembled in 1996 to review the national intelligence estimate (NIE 95–19) on the ballistic-missile threat concluded that not enough attention was being devoted to the possibility that LACMs could be launched from ships to threaten the US homeland. 'Intel Official Defends Threat Estimate', *Inside Missile Defense*, vol. 2, no. 25, 11 December 1996, pp. 1, 10–14.

[47] Dennis M. Gormley, 'Transfer Pathways for Cruise Missiles', in *Report of the Commission to Assess the Ballistic Missile Threat'*, Appendix III, pp. 133–140.

[48] Tanks, *Assessing the Cruise Missile Puzzle*, p. 19.

[49] K. Scott McMahon, 'Unconventional Nuclear, Biological, and Chemical Weapons Delivery Methods: Whither the "Smuggled Bomb"', *Comparative Strategy*, vol 15, no. 2, April–June 1996, pp. 123–24.

[50] For a useful background treatment of homeland-defence challenges, see Michael Sirak and Daniel G. Dupont, 'Experts: US Not Prepared for Cruise Missile Attacks', *Inside Missile Defense*, vol. 4, no. 26, 23 December 1998, pp. 1, 13–15.

[51] As noted in Delaney, 'Air Defense of the United States', p. 184, a false alarm is when a false indication of attack is sent to the National Command Authority, not when a false detection of an

unidentified air vehicle is made.

[52] For details see 'NORAD Working on ACTD Proposal for National Cruise Missile Defense', *Defense Daily*, vol. 209, no. 36, 8 February 2001, p. 1. The article notes that NORAD submitted another proposal for national cruise-missile defence for Fiscal Year 2001 funding but was rejected by the Pentagon.

[53] This estimate is based in part on knowing the costs of theatre air defences together with information gathered in interviews in January 2001.

[54] On the 1998 study, see Sirak and Dupont, 'Experts', pp. 13–15. Knowledge of the 2000 study is based on interviews with participants in December 2000.

Chapter 5

[1] Rarely do missile-defence advocates (whether from government or defence industry) address non-proliferation policy. To the extent that they do, they tend to assume that the MTCR will have no appreciable effect on missile transfers, nor will it be strengthened to improve existing controls. See, for example, Tanks, *Assessing the Cruise Missile Puzzle*. Arms controllers, on the other hand, gravitate towards promoting a new treaty that would greatly improve the MTCR's voluntary controls. See, for example, Jonathan Dean, 'Step-by-step Control over Ballistic and Cruise Missiles', *Disarmament Diplomacy*, no. 31, October 1998 (www.nyu.edu/globalbeat/nuclear/Jdean1098.html).

[2] *Scud* fingerprints are all over the following programmes: North

Korea's *No-Dong* and *Taepo-Dong* 1 and 2; Pakistan's *Ghauri*; Iran's *Shihab*; and Iraq's *Al-Husseyn*.

[3] China has also provided MTCR-restricted items to Pakistan (M-11 missiles) and Iran (technology and equipment). See Robert Shuey and Shirley A. Kan, 'Chinese Missile and Nuclear Proliferation: Issues for Congress', Congressional Research Service Issue Brief IB92056 (Washington DC: US Library of Congress, 6 July 1995); and Tim McCarthy, 'China's Missile Sales – Few Changes for the Future', *Jane's Intelligence Review*, December 1992, pp. 559–63.

[4] See Richard Speier, 'Can the Missile Technology Control Regime Be Repaired?' in Joseph Cirincione (ed.), *Repairing the Regime* (Washington DC: Routledge, 2000), p. 206.

[5] For details see 'Fact Sheet: The Missile Technology Control Regime (MTCR)', Office of Public Affairs, US Arms Control and Disarmament Agency, Washington DC, May 1993. For a more readable treatment of the MTCR, see 'Commonly Asked Questions on the Missile Technology Control Regime', Fact Sheet, Bureau of Nonproliferation, US Department of State, Washington DC, 8 February 2000 (www.state.gov/www/global/arms/np/mtcr/questions.html).

[6] In 1991 the National Academy of Sciences (NAS) conducted an exhaustive study of US export-control policies, using a set of general prerequisites to judge effectiveness. Those used here are modified versions of a broader set of criteria used in the NAS study. See National

Academy of Sciences, *Finding Common Ground: US Export Control in a Changed Global Environment* (Washington DC: National Academy Press, 1991), p. 113. For a more systematic treatment of the MTCR's effectiveness, see McMahon and Gormley, *Controlling the Spread of Land-Attack Cruise Missiles*, chapter 4.

7   See Alexander A. Pikayev, Leonard S. Spector, Elina V. Kirichenko and Ryan Gibson, *Russia, the US and the Missile Technology Control Regime*, Adelphi Paper 317 (London: Oxford University Press for IISS, 1997).

8   Speier, 'Can the Missile Technology Control Regime Be Repaired?' p. 209.

9   Ivan Safronov, 'Iran Demands Weapons', *Moscow Kommersant*, 15 March 2001, p. 10 (FBIS translated text).

10 Speier, 'Can the Missile Technology Control Regime Be Repaired?' p. 215.

11 Both the Chinese and US statements can be found at www.ceip.org/files/projects/npp/resources/PRCStatement112100.htm. For a more thorough analysis of the implications, see Dennis Gormley, 'Place Equal Focus on Cruise Component of Missile Threat', *Defense News*, 29 January 2001, p. 15.

12 Vivek Raghuvanshi, 'India Targets Middle Eastern Market', *Defense News*, 19 March 2001, p. 1. The Indian Defence Ministry reportedly considers Iran a strategic partner with strong 'possibilities and potential for bilateral cooperation'; initial export opportunities to Iran would likely be limited to improvements of existing Iranian systems. Israel is reportedly interested in purchasing 20–30 *Lakshya* target drones, which also can be used as LACMs. See Patrick Brunet, 'India Improves Its Range of Drones', *Air & Cosmos*, 2 March 2001, p. 37 (FBIS translated text).

13 The US transferred the 37-km range *Honest John* rocket to Taiwan and South Korea and the 130km range *Lance* ballistic missile to Israel. No US transfers have occurred since the mid-1970s. Its most controversial UAV transfer was of the 2,250km range *Scarab* to Egypt in the late 1980s.

14 France reportedly transferred MD-660 ballistic missiles to Israel in 1968. They are thought to be the basis for Israel's 500km-range *Jericho* 1 ballistic missiles. See Seth Carus, *Ballistic Missiles in the Third World* (New York: Praeger, 1990), p. 17.

15 See McMahon and Gormley, *Controlling the Spread of Land-Attack Cruise Missiles*, pp. 76–80. There was a slight improvement during Clinton's second term in office, largely because of the inclusion of cruise-missile defence in the administration's counter-proliferation activities.

16 McMahon and Gormley, *Controlling the Spread of Land-Attack Cruise Missiles*, pp. 50–51.

17 See the text of President Bush's Press Conference on 28 December 2000 announcing his nomination of Donald Rumsfeld as Secretary of Defense: www.nytimes.com/2000/12/28/politics/28BUSH-TEXT.html. Donald Rumsfeld first noted his concern about cruise-missile proliferation in the executive summary of his July 1998 report on the ballistic-missile threat. See

Report of the Commission to Assess the Ballistic Missile Threat to the United States, p. 1.

[18] Frederick J. Hollinger, 'The Missile Technology Control Regime: A Major New Arms Control Achievement', in US Arms Control and Disarmament Agency, *World Military Expenditures and Arms Transfers 1987* (Washington DC: USGPO, 1988), p. 26.

[19] Reportedly, in a 2 December 1997 memorandum on the *Black Shaheen* sale, the Chief of Staff to the French Defence Minister, Alain Richard, argued that the missile had a range of around 500km and that there were many reasons to veto the sale. See 'Proliferation: How Paris Arms the UAE', *Intelligence Newsletter*, no. 398, 23 January 2001, p. 6.

[20] Douglas Barrie and Colin Clark, 'Cruise Missile Worries Spark MTCR Action', *Defense News*, 24 July 2000, p. 1.

[21] DeSantis and McKay, *Unmanned Aerial Vehicles*, pp. 32–3.

[22] For a critical appraisal of the issue of expanded membership, see Speier, 'Can the Missile Technology Control Regime Be Repaired?' Also see Victor Zaborsky and Scott Jones (eds), *Missile Proliferation and MTCR: The Nth Member and Other Challenges* (Athens, GA: Center for International Trade and Security, University of Georgia, 1997).

[23] The MTCR's coverage of flight-control systems and technology is provided under Item 10 of Category II, but it constrains only those systems 'designed or modified for the systems in Item 1'. The original 1987 version of Item 10 applied more liberal language – 'usable in the systems

in Item 1' – which might have captured such systems for case-by-case review.

[24] For example, a full array of approaches for preventing UAVs being adapted into MTCR-controlled cruise missiles should be examined. The use of so-called 'safeguards' that preclude conversion of a missile through the use of electronic tamper-proof controls or electronic 'handshakes' certainly deserve study, but they should not be viewed as a rationale for deciding to make frequent exceptions to Category I controls on cruise missiles. It is ludicrous to assume that all MTCR partners could implement uniformly solid and verifiable safeguards, including encryption and code-protection measures to prevent end-user tampering. For a discussion on safeguards for space-launch vehicles, see Brian G. Chow, *Emerging National Space Launch Programs: Economics and Safeguards*, RAND/R-4179-USDP (Santa Monica, CA: RAND Corporation, 1993).

[25] Manufacturers tend to express a cruise missile's range using a low flight profile so as to emphasise defence penetration. Based on the author's experience of attending numerous international arms shows, it is clear that manufacturers are quite sensitive to MTCR controls, and so are prone to describe system capabilities in such a way that they fall below MTCR range and payload thresholds.

[26] It should be noted that only gas-turbine engines, the predominant engines used in cruise missiles, achieve such fuel efficiency at higher altitudes. Also important is the fact that stealthy cruise

missiles, like the Anglo-French *Storm Shadow*, can afford to fly at higher altitudes for longer distances (US stealth aircraft routinely operate at medium altitudes in the presence of enemy air defences).

[27] Besides using altitude to maximise range, the rules should consider the effects of atmosphere, speed, range/fuel/payload trade-offs, simple range/payload trade-offs, whether or not command or internal guidance is used, the effects of dispensable components and combinations thereof.

[28] Since most of these factors are system-specific, each cruise-missile or UAV export would require independent evaluation. That said, even for ballistic missiles, members are already obligated to consider the scope for trading off range and payload – a system-specific evaluation.

[29] See McMahon and Gormley, *Controlling the Spread of Land-Attack Cruise Missiles*, pp. 80–83.

[30] The synergistic benefits of employing countermeasures on stealthy UAVs to enhance penetration is discussed in William A. Schoneberger, 'Backfitting Stealth', *Journal of Electronic Defense*, vol. 21, no. 3, March 1998, pp. 33–7.

[31] These proposals are usefully explored in Richard H. Speier, 'A Nuclear Nonproliferation Treaty for Missiles?' in Henry Sokolski (ed.), *Fighting Proliferation: New Concerns for the Nineties* (Maxwell Air Force Base, AL: Air University Press, 1996), pp. 57–72. Critics of such proposals, including Speier, argue that such treaties could dangerously backfire through making concessions to 'have-not' states that permit the sharing of space-launch vehicle technology, which represents a straightforward route to ballistic-missile acquisition.

Conclusion

[1] See Max Hastings and Simon Jenkins, *The Battle for the Falklands* (New York: Norton, 1983), pp. 153–54, 316–20.

[2] Thomas E. Ricks, 'Pentagon Study May Bring Big Shake-up', *Washington Post*, 9 February 2001, p. 1.

[3] Greg Jaffe, 'Pentagon Lists Potential Cuts in About 30 Weapons Programs', *Wall Street Journal*, 26 March 2001, p. 1.

[4] Rather than leaving funding responsibility for cruise-missile defence with each of the services, it may be necessary to give the BMDO – appropriately retitled – responsibility for both ballistic- and cruise-missile defence programmes.